As one of the world's longest established and best-known travel brands, Thomas Cook are the experts in travel.

For more than 135 years our guidebooks have unlocked the secrets of destinations around the world, sharing with travellers a wealth of experience and a passion for travel.

Rely on Thomas Cook as your travelling companion on your next trip and benefit from our unique heritage.

Thomas Cook **traveller** guides

NORTHEAST FRANCE
Sarah Thorowgood

Your travelling companion since 1873

Thomas Cook

Written by Sarah Thorowgood
Original photography by Mark Bassett

Published by Thomas Cook Publishing
A division of Thomas Cook Tour Operations Limited
Company registration no. 3772199 England
The Thomas Cook Business Park, Unit 9, Coningsby Road,
Peterborough PE3 8SB, United Kingdom
Email: books@thomascook.com, Tel: +44 (0) 1733 416477
www.thomascookpublishing.com

Produced by Cambridge Publishing Management Limited
Burr Elm Court, Main Street, Caldecote CB23 7NU
www.cambridgepm.co.uk

ISBN: 978-1-84848-474-0

First edition © 2011
Text © Thomas Cook Publishing
Maps © Thomas Cook Publishing/PCGraphics (UK) Limited
Transport map © Communicarta Limited

Series Editor: Karen Beaulah
Production/DTP: Steven Collins

Printed and bound in Spain by GraphyCems

Cover photography © Ian Shaw/Alamy

Contents

Introduction

Packed in between the North Sea, Paris and the borders of Belgium, Luxembourg and Germany, the northeast of France is a busy part of the world. Its fertile land and superb connections with eastern and northern Europe as well as Britain mean that it's always been sought-after territory and something of a cosmopolitan European crossroads. With that have come wealth and war in equal measure, both leaving their marks – for better or worse – across the land.

Although the northern edge of a huge country, it's hard not to feel like you are in the middle of something when you visit this region. Its business-like, hard-working attitude is a symptom of centuries of industry in the area: from the wool trade of the 13th century that helped fund the big cities like Lille, as well as a spectacular display of Gothic prowess in cathedrals like Amiens, Beauvais, Reims, Metz and Strasbourg, to the coal mining that powered France's industrial revolution. And the area has been important politically as well as economically: Reims, which saw the coronation of 25 kings, was the symbol of the French monarchy's right to rule, and now Strasbourg, capital of Alsace (a region with an ambiguous border territory identity), plays host to the European Parliament once a month.

Now that Eurostar has put Lille within an hour and a half of London, and the high-speed TGV train service has linked most of the towns in the region to Paris, people are starting to explore the area like never before. The region's industrial image (on the wane since World War II anyway) is starting to give way to a service industry based on the cultural, historical and natural assets that the area has in spades.

It's not an exaggeration to say that all of the region's major cities have something spectacular to offer: from the flawless urban planning of Nancy's Place Stanislas to the technicolour stained glass of Metz's cathedral, or from some of the world's most expensive wine in the champagne cellars of Reims to possibly the best seafood to be had in all France at Lille. And if you want to explore the countryside you'll find plenty to enchant you in the vineyard-clad valleys of Alsace, the snowy peaks of the Vosges mountains or the forests of Picardy and the Ardennes.

But it is perhaps in the reminders of the two world wars of the 20th century that you can most clearly see the region's value reflected. Some visit to explore the vast network of the Maginot Line fortifications along the border with Germany, others come to see for themselves the horror wrought by World War I around the Somme and at places like Verdun. What is certainly true is that they are all sobering reminders of the price that this land, and the people who fought to defend it, paid for its liberty.

Vineyards stretch across swathes of northeast France's countryside

Introduction

The land

The northeast part of France covered in this guide is a big area spanning five official regions and, like the rest of the country, is very varied in its geography. But from the vast, fertile rolling plains of Picardy and Champagne to the gentle, sheltered slopes of the vineyards south of Reims and on the Alsace side of the Vosges mountains, this land has always been productive: its mineral, agricultural and viticultural industries are writ large across the landscape.

Nord-Pas-de-Calais

The smallest of the regions, Nord (as it is generally known) encompasses the old provinces of Flanders and Artois. Squashed up between the North Sea and the border with Belgium, its east coast strongly resembles that of its neighbouring low countries with its flat, marshy and fertile land reclaimed from the sea over centuries. To the west, the chalky cliffs around Cap Gris Nez and Cap Blanc Nez provide you with a cross-sectional geology lesson: this is the chalk plateau that stretches far inland (and was originally the same chunk of land as that which makes up the white cliffs of Dover), its plains providing more arable land. Further east are the lush wooded pastures of the Monts de Flandres, a slightly hillier region that is perfect for livestock. Around Lille and Douai, a bleak sprawling and unremittingly flat industrial landscape emerges, marked with vast slag heaps from a now-defunct coal-mining industry.

Picardy

Picardy covers a bigger area than Nord (comprising the *départements* of Somme, Ainse and Oise) and has a little more variety, but it's essentially a rolling, chalky landscape cut through with rivers and dotted with woodland and, around Compiègne, vast forests. Much of it is the domain of agro-industry on a vast scale, its golden fields of cereal crops seeming to stretch to the horizon and beyond. The region's rivers – the Somme, Oise and Ainse – also shape the landscape, providing much-needed fertile silt, verdant shaded valleys and, on the coast where the Somme meets the sea, Europe's biggest tidal estuary and a haven for birdlife. North of the Somme and south of the Canche river lies a silted-up region of sand dunes and salt marsh naturally reclaimed from the sea and river estuaries that is now part of the Marquenterre bird sanctuary. It's also used to graze cattle highly prized for their unusual salty flavour.

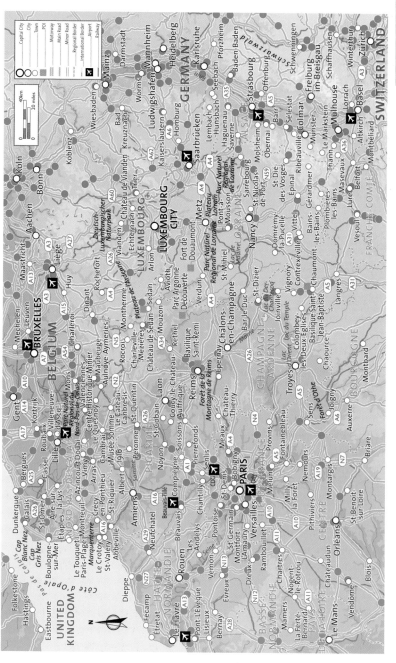

The land

Cap Blanc Nez's dramatic profile

Champagne-Ardenne

Part of the Paris basin, sparsely populated Champagne (comprising the *départements* of Aube, Haute-Marne and Marne) is a low-lying area that millions of years ago was under water. Its broad, open landscape is now, like Picardy to the west, much taken up with large-scale arable farming on its chalky land. South of Reims, this chalk pushes upwards to form the Montage de Reims area, whose gentle and sheltered slopes have proved a goldmine for wine producers ever since they started experimenting with sparkling wine. The multi-million-euro champagne industry has shaped the landscape here and along the banks of the river Marne to the south, with every spare acre of land given over to the ordered lines of vineyards dotted here and there with small, business-like little villages tending their precious crop. To the north, the Ardenne *département* has much more in common with its Belgian namesake, its dark, wooded and hilly land a place of escape from the rat race.

Lorraine

Bordering no fewer than three countries (Belgium, Luxembourg and Germany), Lorraine (comprising the *départements* of Meurthe-et-Moselle, Meuse, Moselle and Vosges) is something of a geographical as well as political crossroads province. In the west, the Paris basin extends into the province, providing more flat and fertile farmland fed by the various meandering rivers that give their names to the region's *départements*, but to the east, the Vosges mountains, gradually climbing up to their highest peaks at around 1,400m (4,595ft), mark a natural boundary shared with Alsace. To the south, the thermal spas around Vittel on the Vosges plateau have their origins in the mountain streams.

Alsace

Protected from the prevailing westerly and southwesterly winds by the Vosges mountains, the thin north–south strip of land that constitutes Alsace (comprising the *départements* of Bas-Rhin and Haut-Rhin) has a much drier climate than the rest of the northeast region. It's one of many differences you will find here. The mountains have cut the area off from the rest of France and somehow seem to force the province to look eastwards to Germany rather than westwards to the centre of France. The craggy and more sharply sloping mountainsides are covered in Alpine firs and mountain pastures that give way suddenly to vineyards as soon as the altitude and temperature allow. Running parallel to the mountains to the east lies the river Rhine, an important waterway still and a definitive border between France and Germany.

The land

The typically picturesque Alsatian village of Riquewihr

History

c. **300** BC	Belgae tribe lives in the northern part of the region known to Romans as Gaul.
c. **58–52** BC	Roman conquest of much of northeast France takes place with varying amounts of local resistance. Over the next hundred years or so, Reims, Metz, Strasbourg, Amiens and Bologne all become important outposts of the Roman province of Belgium.
3rd–5th centuries AD	Succession of invasions of the region by various Germanic tribes follows the collapse of the Roman Empire.
486–511	Merovingian king Clovis manages to unite west Germanic Frankish tribes and takes control of most of the area constituting present-day France. Around 500 AD he converts to Christianity and is baptised by the Bishop of Reims (later Saint Remi) in the old cathedral.
6th–7th centuries	Clovis' conversion turns out to be an important moment for Christianity in the region and several cathedrals and churches are built over the next two centuries. Meanwhile, the Merovingian dynasty falls into decline.
800	Charlemagne, son of Pepin, a leader who had pulled together the disintegrating Merovingian territories, revives the concept of the Roman Empire and is crowned 'Emperor of the Romans' and the Carolingian Empire spans most of western Europe.
816	Charlemagne dies and Louis I, his son, becomes the first of a line of kings to be crowned at Reims. The empire is divided up, in accordance with Charlemagne's wishes, between Louis' sons.
843	The treaty of Verdun officially ratifies an agreement giving each son a separate kingdom: *Francia Media* (including parts of west Germany, eastern northeast France, Belgium and the

Netherlands); *Francia Orientalis* (territories east of the Rhine); *Francia Occidentalis* (the rest of present-day France). This division of land can still be seen to this day and the treaty has even been blamed by some for both World War I and World War II.

Late 9th–10th centuries Some of the three kingdoms are subdivided into smaller dukedoms such as Lotharingia (roughly equivalent to today's Lorraine region) and Alsace, thus weakening the Carolingian Empire. By the end of the 10th century, the Capetian Dynasty is in the ascendant.

11th–13th centuries The relative stability brought about by the Capetian rule and slow reacquisition of most of what is northeast France, largely through a process of diplomacy and intermarriage, sees a period of great prosperity throughout the region. Wealth from the wool trade in the north and trading with neighbouring countries, as well as being something of a communication nexus

between north and south Europe, all contribute to important building projects, including many of the cathedrals still standing today.

1337–1453 The Hundred Years War is fought out across Flanders and Picardy as the English, already now ruling much of western France, vie for control of the rest of the French territory. Battles such as Crécy (1346) and Aquitaine (1415) mark victories for the English but, ultimately, they are defeated in all of France except for Calais. Charles VII is crowned king of France at Reims in 1429, thanks to Joan of Arc.

Late 15th–mid-16th centuries Fringe parts of the region are still either independent areas (like parts of Alsace) or under outside control. The Habsburgs have Flanders and Artois, and Lorraine becomes an independent duchy nominally under the overlordship of the Holy Roman Emperor. Meanwhile, the Renaissance sees a period of flourishing academic and artistic achievement.

1562–98 The Wars of Religion, a symptom to some extent of the fragile political framework of France, and of the warring Catholic and Protestant factions in the rest of Europe, cause havoc across the region, pitting Catholics against Huguenot Protestants.

17th century The Thirty Years War involving prolonged fighting and subsequent peace treaties with the Habsburg Empire ends with the incorporation of Artois, Flanders and Alsace into the Kingdom of France.

1739–66 Stanislas Leszczynski, former king of Poland, is made Duke of Lorraine on the condition that the duchy reverts to the French crown on his death. The region enjoys a golden age of building under his rule.

1789–1815 The French Revolution and rise and fall of Napoleon see further conflict across the region.

19th century France is ruled by a succession of reinstated monarchs and then by the dictator Napoleon III (1848–52), nephew of Napoleon Bonaparte. This second empire comes to an end with his defeat at Sedan in the Franco–Prussian (German) War (1870–71). Alsace and northern Lorraine are annexed by Germany.

1871–1914 A programme of 'Germanification' takes place in Alsace and northern Lorraine. 'Imperial', or 'German', quarters are built in Metz and Strasbourg; the use of French is outlawed. Many people leave the region. Nancy welcomes many intellectuals and artist refugees and sees the blossoming of its Art Nouveau school.

1914–18 World War I sees whole swathes of the region from the Somme, across the Marne to Verdun, locked in a hopeless trench war. Eventual German surrender comes with the signing of the Armistice in the Forêt de Compiègne.

1930s André Maginot oversees the construction of the defensive barrier along the border with Germany, which ultimately proves to be useless.

1940–45   Germany invades France via Belgium and down into the Ardennes. Alsace and north Lorraine again become officially 'German'. Charles de Gaulle orchestrates a resistance movement that contributes to the defeat of the Germans by 1945. This time the Armistice is signed in Reims.

1950s   Post-war reconstruction is carried out in towns across the region and the Council of Europe headquarters is located in Strasbourg.

1960s–70s   Decline of the mining industry leads to a decimation of the regional economy and unemployment from which northeast France is only now beginning to recover.

1990s   The Channel Tunnel is opened in 1994, bringing a renewed sense of optimism to Nord-Pas-de-Calais and Picardy. There is extensive redevelopment in towns across the region, including Amiens, where restoration

work on the cathedral reveals the original brilliant colours of its façade. Strasbourg becomes, along with Brussels and Luxembourg, 'capital' of the European Union.

2000   A foiled Islamic fundamentalist plot to blow up Strasbourg's cathedral foreshadows a decade of turbulence and fear of Islamic terrorism throughout the world.

2004   Lille becomes European Capital of Culture and sees a big upturn in tourism as a result of the Eurostar.

2005   President Jacques Chirac reopens Place Stanislas in Nancy after a €9 million restoration programme.

2007   The TGV brings Strasbourg (and Metz and Nancy) within two and a half hours of Paris.

May 2010   Metz takes centre stage on the European cultural scene with the opening of the Centre Pompidou Metz, the largest temporary exhibition space in France outside Paris.

Politics

France is a republic with both an elected president as head of state and a prime minister chosen by the president. The current president, Nicolas Sarkozy, is head of the right-of-centre Union pour un Mouvement Populaire (UMP, Union for a Popular Movement), one of four main parties in the country. The others are the left-wing Parti Socialiste (PS, Socialist Party) and Parti Communiste Français (PCF, French Communist Party) and the liberal-centrist Mouvement Démocrate (MoDem, Democratic Movement).

Until 1982, virtually all political power in the country resided in Paris with the Sénat (Senate, upper parliamentary house) and Assemblée Nationale (National Assembly, lower house). Local *départements* (there are 96 in total in France) were run by a prefect, appointed by the central government, and a locally elected council, the Conseil Général. But legislation brought in since the early 1980s has slowly shifted power towards the regions, giving locally elected officials (there are 22 regions in France), the *départements*, and below that the *communes* (about 36,000 in total) more and more administrative and fiscal power. With responsibility for tourism (one of France's biggest and fastest-growing industries) as well as for other industrial development, the regions have, generally speaking, thrived under this new system, which has allowed them to promote themselves to businesses across Europe without interference from central government.

The tourism sector has also benefited hugely from this devolution of power. Responsibility for education also lies at a regional level and the *départements* oversee welfare and social services.

The region covered in this book is varied in its political make-up: Alsace, for example, is traditionally seen as a conservative region, while Picardy and Nord-Pas-de-Calais are generally considered a heartland of the working-class left. But in the 2007 elections, the race for the presidency was a close run. The Nord *département*, for example, narrowly voted for Sarkozy over Ségolène Royal of the Parti Socialiste, and the far-right Front National (FN) gained 16 per cent in Pas-de-Calais (immigration and the infamous Sangatte refugee camp near Calais almost certainly having something to do with these local anomalies).

Given that the presidential term of office is five years, the next elections will be held in 2012 and at the time of writing it looks very possible that

Nicolas Sarkozy will not be re-elected. Despite a wave of optimism for his can-do, right-wing *libéralisme* politics, he has faced huge problems tackling the unions and left-wing elements of the Assemblée Nationale and his popularity rating with the French public in general has reached an all-time low. General strikes took place across the country in autumn 2010 in protest at his government's response to the budget deficit and at general austerity measures being implemented across the entire European Union as a result of the global financial crisis. Sarkozy has also been personally criticised by other political leaders in France and across Europe for his role in the expulsions of Roma from the country, which took place in the summer of 2010.

Politics

The Louise Weiss building in Strasbourg: official seat of the European Parliament

Culture

Lovers of culture – in all its forms – will be richly rewarded in this region of France. The cradle of Gothic architecture from the 13th to the 15th century and with a host of grand 17th- and 18th-century civic buildings, northern France has a long and venerable architectural heritage still being tested by innovative new building projects like the Centre Pompidou-Metz.

The area's myriad museums are especially well stocked with 17th-century Flemish and Dutch masters, and all of the region's cities have theatres, opera houses and concert halls (*see pp151–3*) that supply a culture-hungry population with a varied programme of classical music, theatre, ballet and contemporary dance.

Architecture

The first thing that will strike you about any reasonable-sized town in the area will almost certainly be its church. Thanks in part to wealth from the lucrative wool trade in the 12th and 13th centuries – and the sale of indulgences, which were essentially a sort of monetary penance – Gothic architecture from Île de France and Paris spread throughout the region and found its apogée in buildings like the cathedrals of Amiens, Soissons, Beauvais, Reims, Metz and Strasbourg, all of which in their different ways are outstanding examples of the style. And the trend filtered down to smaller buildings too, the result being the huge number of Gothic churches to be found all over the region. All that wealth also built plenty of civic and private buildings over the 16th, 17th and 18th centuries: from the 16th-century Renaissance town houses of Troyes and the 17th-century Grand'Place in Lille to the neoclassical perfection of town squares like Place Stanislas in Nancy and Place Royale in Reims. Alsace, however, that bit removed from the French architectural traditions happening further west in the 16th and 17th centuries before it became part of France, has a different feel to it, most notable in its pointed, ornate gables and innovative oriel windows. Miraculously, despite two devastating world wars in the last century, there is still a lot to see, but the damage caused by World War I also allowed new styles to develop and you will find quite a lot of both Art Nouveau (circa 1890–1905) and Art Deco (1920s and 1930s) buildings, especially in Nancy and Reims, respectively. Metz's 'Imperial', or 'German', quarter near the station is another architecturally important urban area that was applying for UNESCO World Heritage status at the time of writing. It's an extraordinary hotchpotch of styles: neo-Romanesque and neoclassical is mixed with some Art Nouveau and Art Deco, as well as bizarre mock-Bavarian buildings that were designed to put an emphatic German stamp on the annexed town. More recently, one of the most talked-about buildings in France – the other-worldly form of the Centre Pompidou-

Metz designed by Japanese architect Shigeru Ban with Jean de Gastines – was unveiled to universal critical acclaim in May 2010.

Art

Much of the artistic talent of northeast France was bound up with the construction of the great cathedrals – all of which needed stone carvings and sculptures for their increasingly ornate western façades and portals, and illustrative stained glass for their increasingly large windows. Many of these sculptural masterpieces are now often displayed inside museums –

Culture

Lille's opera house on the Baroque Place du Théâtre

The cathedral's vaulted ceiling, in Amiens

see some of the vast output of the influential Daum factory in the Musée des Beaux-Arts and at the Musée de L'École de Nancy.

Perhaps the most famous sculptors to come from this part of the world are the Renaissance-era Ligier Richier, based in Saint-Mihiel in Lorraine, some of whose greatest work can be seen in that town's churches as well as in museums and galleries across Lorraine; Frédéric Auguste Bartholdi, who was from Colmar and is most famous for his Statue of Liberty, which now adorns New York Harbour; and Jean (Hans) Arp, part of the 20th-century avant-garde, much of whose work is displayed in his home town of Strasbourg.

Literature

Given that the printing press was largely devised in Strasbourg by Johannes Gutenberg in the 15th century, it comes as little surprise that the region has an impressive literary tradition. But about three centuries before anything was printed, Chrétien de Troyes was taking the courts of Champagne and Flanders by storm with his tales of adventure and chivalry. A *trouvère* (or *troubadour*, as they were known in southern France), he wrote several long poems in rhyming couplets, including the story of Lancelot and that of Perceval and the Holy Grail. His works were hugely influential on the rest of Western literature and he has even been credited with being the inventor of the modern novel.

partly for fear that acidic rain will ruin them, and partly also so that visitors can view the extraordinary artistic mastery and detail close up. Stained-glass producers from Reims, Troyes and Metz supplied the huge demand for glass from all of the region's churches, and in Reims, the Simon family, whose workshop was established in 1640, is still making glass 12 generations later. Much of the modern glass you see in Reims' cathedral comes from here, but the 20th-century Russian émigré Marc Chagall was also a noted master craftsman in this field and his work can be seen both here and in Metz's cathedral. Glassware also became an important part of the Art Nouveau movement, and in Nancy you can still

Jean de la Fontaine, as every French schoolchild will tell you, is another important figure in the French literary tradition. He came from Château-Thierry in southern Picardy and in the 17th century wrote many books of fables that are still being read at bedtime to this day.

The towering 18th-century Enlightenment figure Voltaire lived about 100km (62 miles) east of Troyes, at Cirey-sur-Blaise on the border of Champagne and Lorraine, with Émilie du Châtelet, a great thinker in her own right. While here, between them, they made a significant contribution to the worlds of philosophy, science and literature.

Finally, poet Arthur Rimbaud was born in Charleville in the Ardennes, and despite running away from what he thought of as the stifling provinciality of the region, first to Paris and then further afield, he returned here often throughout his short life. Much of his work was inspired by the area and written while he was still a very young man and living here. *Le Bateau Ivre* (*The Drunken Boat*), one of his most powerful and well-known poems, was composed while looking out across the river.

sidebar
Culture

Contemporary art and sculpture at the Centre Pompidou-Metz

Festivals

From Christmas through to the autumn grape harvests, the region abounds with festivals and events. Throughout the summer, you will find it hard to avoid them – especially if you are travelling around small villages at the weekends. From traditional festivals celebrating elements of the Christian calendar such as the Assumption (15 August) through to internationally renowned and cutting-edge celebrations of contemporary music, the sheer variety of events mirrors the richness of the region's culture.

Cultural festivals (music and performing arts)

Strasbourg's classical musical festival, **Festival de Musique de Strasbourg** (*www.festival-strasbourg.com*), takes place over three weeks in June. It's been running for over 70 years and attracts performers (and listeners) from around the world. The city also hosts a contemporary classical music festival **Musica** (*www.festivalmusica.org*) in late September and early October. For a month from mid-June to mid-July in Reims, meanwhile, **Les Flâneries Musicales de Reims** (*www.flaneriesreims.com*) is another well-known event on the international (mainly classical) music scene.

The **Jazz Festival** at Amiens (*www.amiens jazzfestival.com*) is another highlight for international music in the region and is held in the last week of March. Since 1980, Colmar has also held a highly regarded international classical music festival, **Festival International de Colmar** (*www.festival-colmar.com*) in

the first two weeks of July. Troyes' **Nuits de Champagne** (*www.nuitsde champagne.com*) is an important celebration of the voice and songwriting, showcasing everything from classical choral to rock, folk and blues for a week at the end of October.

Charleville-Mézières's **Festival Mondial des Théâtres de Marionnettes** (World Puppetry Theatre Festival, *www.festival-marionnette.com*) is a huge and truly international event taking place for one week in mid-September once every three years. Book your tickets well in advance if you want to stay in town at this time.

Wine and food festivals

You will find small wine fairs taking place in all of the wine villages of Alsace throughout the summer (ask at the local tourist office for details) and also on the Saturday or Sunday nearest to the feast day of the patron saint of winegrowers, St

Vincent (22 January). You will also find many other wine producer fairs in cities like Reims, where you will be able to taste hundreds of different champagnes (again, tourist offices will have details). In the Ardennes, look out for beer festivals too.

Metz's **Fêtes de la Mirabelle** (Mirabelle Festival, *www.mairie-metz.fr*) celebrates Lorraine's most famous fruit in style at harvest time (late August) each year with floats, music and fireworks. Head to Rethel in the Ardennes in late April for the **Foire au Boudin Blanc** to try the best boudin blanc sausage in France (*www.tourisme-ardennes.com*).

Religious festivals

As well as the wine and harvest fêtes you will see happening in villages across the region, most of these places will also have a local saint's day festival (see local tourist offices for details), which will usually happen on the weekend closest to the actual day. Other important dates in the Christian calendar are: **Mardi Gras** (Shrove Tuesday), for which Strasbourg has an especially big event; **L'Assomption** (15 August); and the Christmas season when the **Fête de Saint Nicolas** (Feast of St Nicholas, 6 December) is celebrated across the region and there are **Christmas markets** in almost all of the big towns and cities.

Strasbourg's town centre, lit up for Christmas

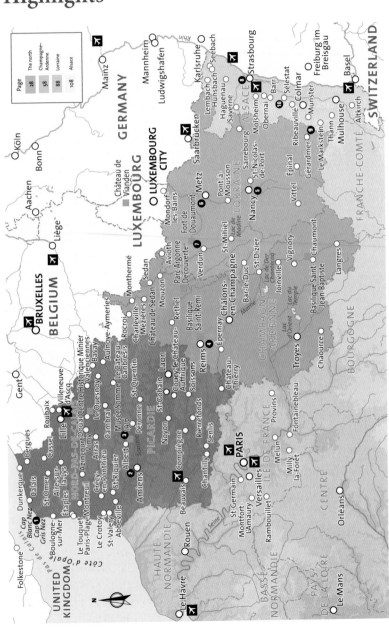

1 Beaches south of Calais (Côte d'Opale) Walking along the windswept GR21 coastal footpath, past the high, chalky cliffs of Gris Nez and Blanc Nez and down to the wide, sweeping sandy beaches, enjoying the vast views of the busy English Channel and England on a clear day (*see pp38–40*).

2 Amiens' Cathédrale Notre-Dame and *hortillonnages* Gazing at the spectacular, light-filled cathedral, perhaps the purest example of 13th-century Gothic brilliance you will find in the whole region, and visiting the *hortillonnages*, the fertile market gardens that still produce fruit and vegetables sold in the town and that offer a picture-postcard view of the cathedral (*see pp51–2*).

3 Battlefields of the Somme Discovering hundreds of stark, thought-provoking and deeply moving reminders of the huge sacrifice of World War I around the town of Arras and along the Somme valley; from the dignified beauty of Lutyens' towering Monument to the Missing at Thiepval to the peaceful solitude of the many small cemeteries you will find in fields and by roadsides (*see pp42–5*).

4 Champagne Tasting multitudes of different labels in countless cellars between Reims and Épernay, from the great, world-renowned champagne houses like Tattinger, Veuve Cliquot-Ponsardin and Moët & Chandon with their cathedral-like *caves*, to lively up-and-coming small producers in the villages of the Montagne de Reims (*see pp68–9*).

5 Place Stanislas, Nancy Drinking in the culture (and perhaps an apéritif or two) in Nancy's spacious and perfectly planned main square, a work of 18th-century neoclassical bravura and the legacy of the enlightened last Duke of Lorraine, Stanislas Leszczyski (*see p95 and box p96*).

6 Centre Pompidou-Metz Exploring the groundbreaking architecture and world-class exhibitions of modern and contemporary art at the most talked-about arrival on the cultural scene of northeast France, the new outpost of the Centre Pompidou in Paris (*see pp92–3*).

7 Battlefield of Verdun Taking in the shocking collection of memorials to the war that raged throughout 1916 just a few kilometres outside Verdun, where whole villages were pounded into oblivion by shells; the ossuary in Douaumont holds the remains of over 130,000 unidentified men – French and German – killed in action here (*see pp100–102*).

8 **Strasbourg centre** Revelling in the busy, modern 'European capital' with its old, well-preserved and picturesque Alsatian heart, which includes a breathtaking cathedral, on an island in the river Ill (*see pp110–13*).

9 **Southern Vosges mountains** Hiking, or driving, through the most spectacular scenery of the entire region. The bluey-grey Vosges mountains and the Route des Crêtes have views east that on a clear day stretch over the broad Rhine valley to the Black Forest in Germany (*see pp133–4*).

10 **Route des Vin** Leisurely sipping and tasting your way along the beautiful Alsatian wine route, a string of pretty villages and busy little towns connected by the manicured landscape of vineyards that produce some increasingly excellent French white wines (*see pp124–5*).

Take a boat trip through the *hortillonnages*, Amiens

Suggested itineraries

The region covered in this book – which constitutes the area roughly from Calais due south to Paris and east across to the Belgian, Luxembourg and German borders – is a large geographical area and there is a lot to see. You could spend weeks here and still only manage to visit half of it, so you are going to have to be selective.

The other thing to bear in mind about this part of the world is that it is not well connected to the UK by air (unless you plan to fly to Paris), so you will almost certainly need to drive or take the train to get here. The good news is that the region is well served by trains and the road network is also excellent.

Long weekend

If you are driving over to France from the UK for a long weekend, don't try to cover too much ground or you will spend most of your time sitting in the car. Over three or four days, however, you could visit Lille (about an hour and a half from Calais) for an afternoon or perhaps spend the night here. On the second day, head south to Arras, Albert and Péronne and perhaps drive the Circuit de Souvenir. Either Arras or Péronne would make a good place to stop for the night. On the third day, you could visit Amiens, or perhaps Compiègne, both of which have enough to occupy you for an afternoon and

evening. Alternatively, you might prefer to get out into the country and walk (or cycle) some of the trails in the Forêt de Compiègne. On your final day, you may have enough time to head to the coast either to visit the Somme estuary or to take a walk along the cliff south of Calais before catching the ferry or Eurotunnel shuttle train home.

If you plan to visit the area by train and not hire a car, you will obviously be more restricted, but Lille is only an hour and a half from London and towns like Amiens are about an hour and a half from Lille Flandres station (which serves most of the towns in the region). Compiègne is three hours from Lille. Alternatively, if you wanted to get further east into Reims or even Metz, Nancy and Strasbourg, you would be better off taking the Eurostar to Paris (which is now two and a half hours from London St Pancras) and then connecting with the TGV (Train de Grande Vitesse, high-speed train). Reims is just 45 minutes from Paris Est station, Metz and Nancy an hour and a half, and Strasbourg two and a quarter hours.

One week

In a week with a car you could see all of the above and then start to get further into the countryside, visiting little villages or heading off the beaten track to places like the Ardennes on the

Rolling fields and world-famous fizz characterise the Champagne region

Belgian border or the lakes in southern Champagne around Troyes. If you want to visit any of the larger towns and cities in the region, allow at least half a day. Places like Reims and Troyes deserve more time – you'd be hard-pressed to see most of their important sights in less than a day. If you are visiting the Champagne wine region, you should allow between a half and a full day to visit the vineyards and other sights between Reims and Épernay. If you plan to go further east still, you could spend a week seeing Metz, Nancy, Verdun and then perhaps a day at a spa, or some time hiking in the Vosges.

Two weeks

Two weeks will give you plenty of time to visit the north, Champagne and then further east into Lorraine and Alsace, but you would still be pushing it to see any of the region in much detail if you covered this much ground. If you want to get a flavour of the whole region and are limited to a couple of weeks, try focusing on a few important cities: for example, Lille, Amiens, Reims, Metz and Nancy, Strasbourg and Colmar, interspersed with nights spent out in the country in between each town. You'd be staying in a different place every night for two weeks, which is tiring, but you'd see a lot and get a real sense of the region's variety and, in some cases, its similarities.

Longer

If you have more than two weeks, take your time. It's always better to spend two nights in a town rather than one if there is plenty to see and do – which is the case with all of the towns mentioned above. You'd also have more time to get out to some wild countryside like the Vosges and go hiking or skiing for a long weekend. Alternatively, why not try enrolling in a cooking or language course?

Lutyens' Memorial to the Missing, on the Somme battlefields, makes for a more sobering experience

The north

Just a hop over the Channel from the white cliffs of Dover and a skip from the Belgium border, the French administrative regions of Nord–Pas-de-Calais and Picardy – which grew rich on the wool trade of the Middle Ages and, later, coal mining and steel production – have always been strategically important and, therefore, have seen more than their fair share of fighting over the centuries.

Today, the flat, open landscape bears the scars in particular of World War I. Its rutted fields to the north of the Somme valley each year throw up an 'iron harvest' of ordnance that serves as a continual reminder of the horror of that time, and its myriad cemeteries and memorials to the dead are visited by many thousands who come to pay homage to the fallen and learn more about the conflict at centres such as Arras, Albert, Péronne and Vimy. But the land was also fertile and prosperous and saw the rise of some very fine cities. Beautiful Flemish Lille, with a Grand'Place to rival that of Brussels, is once again seeing a renaissance in its fortunes after years in the doldrums in the 1970s and '80s, thanks in large part to the advent of Eurostar. And Amiens, capital of Picardy, and Beauvais to the south are home to two of France's finest cathedrals and well worth a weekend of your time.

Finally, there is the coast, a sweeping curve all the way from the Belgian border to the mouth of the river Somme and beyond. Here you'll find dramatic chalky cliffs at Cap Gris Nez and Cap Blanc Nez in the north and wide, sandy beaches and bays south of Boulogne that seem to stretch on forever.

Take in the stunning architecture of Arras' town centre

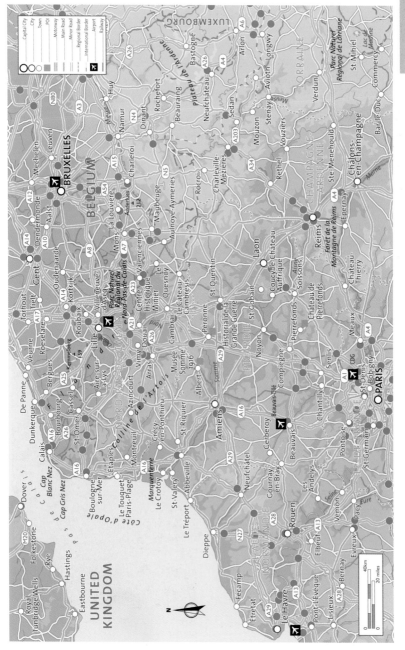

LILLE

A well-positioned port on the river Deûle, and at something of a crossroads in northern Europe, Lille flourished as a merchant city in the Middle Ages despite the waxing and waning fortunes of the various counts (Flanders), dukes (Burgundy) and kings (The Netherlands and France) that possessed her over a period of nearly 700 years. Becoming part of France once and for all in 1713, the city was an important industrial centre in the 19th and 20th centuries. Following the severe industrial decline of the 1970s and '80s, life blood was pumped back into France's fourth-biggest city with the arrival of the TGV and Eurostar. Now just 80 minutes from London, 60 from Paris and 35 from Brussels, Lille is once again the thriving service centre that it was 400 years ago. And tourism to the city is on the up too: its architectural riches span several centuries and styles,

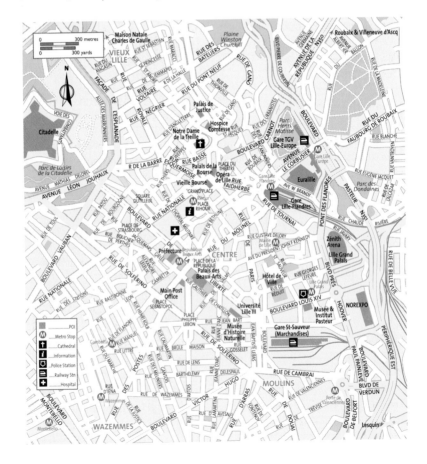

from its splendid 17th-century Flemish Grand'Place, with its Vieille Bourse, to its monumental 19th-century Palais des Beaux-Arts, and its cultural status was revived by a stint as European Capital of Culture in 2004. On top of this, its fine yet distinctively Flemish gastronomic reputation draws diners from towns all over the northeast of France, including Paris, as well as from across the English Channel.

Tourist office, *Palais Rihour, place Rihour. Tel: 08 91 56 20 04. www.lilletourism.com. Open: Mon–Sat 9.30am–6.30pm, Sun & bank holidays 10am–noon & 2–5pm. Closed: 1 Jan, 1 May & 25 Dec.*

Pretty buildings line Lille's Grand'Place

Around Grand'Place and Vieux Lille

Lille's heart is Place Général de Gaulle, more popularly known as **Grand'Place**, and the two squares to the north and south of it: the Baroque **Place du Théâtre** and more modern **Place Rihour**, respectively. This is where Lillois come to meet after work, the broad open spaces scattered with café tables and hurrying commuters.

On the east side of Grand'Place, the **Vieille Bourse**, the city's old stock exchange, is perhaps Lille's most impressively sumptuous building. Built in 1653 by Julien Destrée, its lavishly detailed façade sums up the city's wealth and ambition perfectly and it placed Lille on the Flemish map – in direct competition with the prosperous cities of the Low Countries. These days,

the inner courtyard, housing a second-hand book market, is open every afternoon from Tuesday to Sunday. Tango evenings are also held here on Sundays 7–10pm from July to September (*check with the tourist office for more details*).

Nearby, the remains of the Gothic **Palais Rihour** hark back to the city's Burgundian heritage. The palace was built between 1454 and 1473 by Philip the Good and his son, Charles the Bold, both dukes of Burgundy, and became the town hall following Burgundy's demise in the 17th century. You can visit the Salle des Gardes (which houses the tourist office) and the Salle du Conclave, the former ducal chapel (*Open: Mon–Fri 9am–noon & 2–5pm,*

Striking 17th-century art at the Hospice Comtesse

Sat & Sun 10am–noon & 2–5pm.
Free admission).

North of the Grand'Place is the until-recently crumbling **Vieux Lille** (Old Town), a maze of cobbled streets and passageways that has undergone considerable gentrification in the last decade or so. It's an atmospheric area in which to wander and there are plenty of cafés and bars, as well as chi-chi boutiques, once you've checked out the area's handful of attractions. The **Hospice Comtesse**, a hospital founded in 1237 (although the current buildings date from the 15th, 17th and 18th centuries) and which remained in service until 1939, now houses a collection of 17th-century Flemish art, porcelain and tapestries (*32 rue de la Monnaie. Tel: 03 28 36 84 00. Open: Mon 2–6pm, Wed–Sun 10am–12.30pm*

& 2–6pm. Closed: Tue & some public holidays. Admission charge). The **Maison Natale Charles de Gaulle** (Charles de Gaulle's birthplace) commemorates one of France's most iconic 20th-century figures in the house in which he was born in 1890 (*9 rue Princesse. Tel: 03 28 38 12 05. www.maison-natale-de-gaulle.org. Open: Wed–Sat 10am–1pm & 2–6pm, Sun 1.30–5.30pm. Admission charge).*

Other museums and galleries
LaM

In Villeneuve d'Ascq, what was formerly called the Lille Métropole Musée d'Art Moderne reopened in September 2010 after extensive refurbishment. It is Lille's respected modern art gallery and includes several Cubist, Fauvist and Surrealist

masterpieces by the likes of Picasso, Modigliani and Miró.
Allée du Musée. Tel: 03 20 19 68 68. www.musee-lam.fr. Open: Tue–Sun 10am–6pm. Admission charge.

Palais des Beaux-Arts (Fine Arts Museum)

This is the second-largest museum in France after the Louvre in Paris and houses an impressive collection of paintings, from Flemish old masters like Rubens to some 19th-century French big-hitters such as Monet and Delacroix.
Place de la République. Tel: 03 20 06 78 00. www.pba-lille.fr. Open: Mon 2–6pm, Wed–Sun 10am–6pm. Admission charge.

La Piscine, Musée d'Art et d'Industrie André Diligent (André Diligent Museum of Art and Industry)

Housed in a glorious former Art Deco swimming pool, this applied arts gallery displays work mainly from the late 19th and early 20th century and is well worth the 15km (9¼-mile) trip out of the centre to Roubaix, northeast of Lille.
23 rue de l'Espérance. Tel: 03 20 69 23 60. www.roubaix-lapiscine.com. Open: Tue–Thur 11am–6pm, Fri 11am–8pm, Sat & Sun 1–6pm. Admission charge.

The building alone is enough to justify a visit to Roubaix's art gallery

French Flanders

Like many parts of the vast area of western Europe that makes up modern-day France, French Flanders (the name comes from the Germanic *flauma*, which means 'flooded area') has an identity and flavour all of its own. Now consisting roughly of the *arrondissements* of Lille, Douai and Dunkerque, the region was part of the County of Flanders that spread across The Netherlands, Belgium and northeast France and was one of the most wealthy, powerful and influential regions of Europe.

The first Count of Flanders was Baldwin the First, who was given the title by his father-in-law, the Frankish king Charles the Bald, in 862. Nominally subject to this French feudal overlord, the county exerted considerable independence for centuries as its ports bustled with trading ships bound for England and the Baltic and the money from the hugely lucrative textile industry flowed in. By the 13th century, the region was one of the most densely populated in Europe, its numerous towns busy building drapery halls, churches and belfries as testament to their prosperity. From the 15th to the 17th century, Flanders was ruled first by the Dukes of Burgundy and then became subsumed into the Habsburg Empire as part of the Spanish Netherlands. But despite or perhaps because of this, it retained its distinct Flemishness – an identity that is still visible in French Flanders today. You can see it in place names such as Roubaix, Lille and Dunkerque, in the flat, expansive and watery landscape, in the cafés (known round these parts

The 18th-century wooden windmill at Cassel

Excellent seafood restaurants can be found in Flemish Lille

as *estaminets*) serving *moules-frites* (mussels with French fries) and Pelforth bier, and, perhaps most impressively, in the region's museums, which between them host an impressive haul of Dutch Renaissance paintings. And then there are the windmills: the Noordmeulen just outside the town of Hondschoote, south of Dunkerque and on the border with Belgium, is considered to be Europe's oldest windmill and there are around 40 others still in existence in the area.

Despite having been fully integrated into France by Louis XIV in the 17th century, the people of South Flanders (what is now the French part of Flanders) continued for some time to speak Flemish, a tradition that has been slowly eroded following the increasingly centralised government of France since the Revolution in 1789. These days, Flemish-speakers in the region are a tiny minority: studies conducted in the 1990s suggested that around 20 per cent of people living in French Flanders speak Flemish as their mother tongue but that only 5 per cent of them use the language on a daily basis, and the younger generation are even less likely to speak it. However, pressure groups like the Komitee voor Frans-Vlaanderen (Committee for French Flanders) continue to fight for the language's inclusion in school and university curricula. And French Flemishness is also still very much in evidence in the region's cuisine. As well as the ubiquitous *moules-frites*, you will also see more hearty, northern fare on the menu: *potjevleesch* (a mouth-watering four-meat terrine, usually including veal, pork and sometimes rabbit or chicken); *hochepot* (a rich stew made from various assorted meats and vegetables); *waterzoï* (freshwater fish or chicken in a creamy sauce); and, most famously, *carbonade de beouf* (or pretty much any other kind of meat) *à la flammande* (beef cooked in beer).

NORD-PAS-DE-CALAIS
Aire-sur-la-Lys

A classic small Flemish-Artois town 16km (10 miles) southeast of Saint-Omer, attractive and sleepy Aire sits on the river Lys, a tributary of the Scheldt, which at one point made it a seat of modest importance. Evidence of this can be seen in the splendid Romanesque **Collégiale Saint-Pierre** (Collegiate Church of St Peter), which seems almost too grand for the little place, and the 16th-century Flemish Renaissance **Bailliage** (Bailiwick), once the town hall and now the location of the tourist office. There's also a UNESCO World Heritage-listed **belfry** from which you can survey the town and surrounding plain (*Open: Apr–Sept from 3pm for a 75-minute guided visit. Reservations at the tourist office. Admission charge*).

Cassel

Situated on top of one of the few hills for miles around, Cassel is a treat with its cobbled Flemish Grand'Place and its sweeping views of the plain below from its public gardens that occupy the site where once stood a medieval castle. About 30km (19 miles) south of Dunkerque, its valuable hilltop vantage point was fought over for centuries and the town saw its fair share of action in both world wars (Maréchal Foch was based here at one point and it was fighting here that helped the Allies leave from Dunkerque). You can also visit the **Casteel-Meulen**, a wooden 18th-century windmill that still produces flour and linseed oil (*Tel: 03 28 40 52 55 (tourist office). Open: Apr–Sept 10am–12.30pm & 2–5.30pm. Admission charge*).

Dunkerque

A town forever associated with the evacuation to Britain of 350,000 Allied troops in 1940, it's hardly surprising to find that the industrial port of Dunkerque was largely flattened during World War II. However, its subsequent rebuild could have been a lot worse and the town is not without its charm – and a lively student population. If you are heading to the north coast for a day or two, Dunkerque makes for a more pleasant stay than either of its more prosaic competitors, Calais and

Cassel's cobbled town centre

Boats deck the inner harbour at Dunkerque

Boulogne. As well as **Malo-les-Bains**, a suburb to the east of the centre that was largely untouched by the war and still exudes a belle-époque elegance, there are a couple of museums worth exploring. The **Musée Portuaire**, in an old tobacco warehouse, will get you up to speed with the port's interesting history (*9 quai de la Citadelle. Tel: 03 28 63 33 39. www.museeportuaire.com. Open: Sept–Jun 10am–12.45pm & 1.30–6pm; Jul–Aug 10am–6pm. Admission charge*), and **Lieu d'Art et Action Contemporaine** (literally translated as 'Place of Art and Contemporary Action'), standing in a sculpture park, shows off some interesting contemporary objects (*Jardin de Sculpture. Tel: 03 28 29 56 00. Open: Apr–Oct 10am–12.15pm & 2–6.30pm; Nov–Mar 10am–12.15pm & 2–5.50pm. Admission charge*).

Saint-Omer

Just 45km (28 miles) southeast of Calais, pretty Saint-Omer survived the war unscathed and is worth a stop on your way south to see a few impressive buildings, not least its 12th- to 15th-century Gothic **Basilique Notre-Dame**, considered one of the most beautiful churches in the region, and the **Musée de l'Hôtel Sandelin**, an elegant 18th-century mansion built for the Viscountess of Fruges and now a museum (*14 rue Carnot. Tel: 03 21 38 00 94. Wed–Sun 10am–12pm and 2–6pm. Admission charge*). The latter contains some wonderful Dutch and Flemish paintings, a collection of Delft ceramics and a famous medieval piece of gold and enamel work, the Pied de Croix de Saint-Bertin (the base of the St Bertin Cross).

CÔTE D'OPALE

This windswept and opalescent stretch of coast south from Calais to the mouth of the Somme offers some spectacular chalk cliffs around Cap Blanc Nez and Cap Gris Nez to Boulogne – not unlike those at Dover, a mere 35km (22 miles) away. These uninterrupted sandy beaches house a smattering of pretty seaside towns and fishing ports and, at the mouth of the Canche and Somme rivers, the haunting bird sanctuary at the Parc du Marquenterre (*see p128*).

Boulogne-sur-Mer

A name most commonly associated these days with booze cruises, Boulogne does in fact have a few other attractions that may persuade you to linger a little longer than it takes to perform a quick *supermarché* sweep. The **Ville Haute** is the most charming quarter, with its medieval walls that you can walk around and the domineering 19th-century **Basilique Notre-Dame**. But pride of place in the work-a-day port's tourist guide goes to **Nausicaá**, a mega-aquarium that is the largest sealife

Boulogne-sur-Mer's arresting Italian-style cathedral dome

Sweeping views across the sea from the cliffs at Cap Blanc Nez

centre in Europe (*Boulevard Sainte-Beuve. www.nausicaa.fr. Open: Jul–Aug daily 9.30am–7.30pm; rest of the year daily 9.30am–6.30pm. Closed: 4–22 Jan. Admission charge*). Expect a staggering array of sea life encompassing everything from hammerhead sharks to jellyfish, some mammals and birds (sea lions and penguins), as well as vast crowds of children in the summer months.

Cap Blanc Nez and Cap Gris Nez

These two chalk headlands on either side of the pleasant seaside town of **Wissant** provide bracing cliff-top walks (along the GR21 'littoral') and a perfect lookout point from which to survey the comings and goings in the Channel. The cliffs (and in fact the whole of the coast around here) are dotted with

concrete bunkers (*Blockhäuser*) installed by the Germans during World War II and used as fortified lookout posts. The **tourist office** in Wissant can provide maps and details of walking trails (*Place de la Mairie. www.terredes 2caps.fr*).

Le Touquet and Étaples

Leafy Le Touquet Paris-Plage, to give it its rather fancy official name, and the considerably more down-to-earth fishing port of Étaples, facing it on the other side of the Canche river, lie around 30km (19 miles) south of Boulogne as the crow flies (in fact, you could walk all the way there along the beach from Boulogne if you wanted to). Laid out within a cooling pine forest in the 19th century as a seaside resort for English holidaymakers, Le

Touquet's heyday came in the interwar period, when the likes of Noel Coward and P G Wodehouse summered in its smart villas. These days, it's a cheerful enough place with a beachfront promenade, still popular with Brits, and is reasonably well supplied with places to stay and eat (*see 'Directory'*) and things to do. Children, especially, will warm to the huge water slides of the **Aqualud** swimming complex on the beach (*Tel: 08 25 74 77 07. www.aqualud.com. Open: varies throughout the year but usually 10am–6pm; check website for details. Closed: Oct–Jan. Admission charge*).

Étaples is a pretty little fishing village cashing in on the tourist trade across the river. Aside from wandering round the harbour and fish market, you can take various boat trips to fish or just enjoy the sea (*bookings at the tourist office, La Corderie, Boulevard Bigot Descelers. Tel: 03 21 09 56 94. Open: Apr–Sept*).

Montreuil-sur-Mer

When the river Canche silted up, one-time port Montreuil-sur-Mer lost something of its raison d'être, but it's an appealing place nonetheless and worth a diversion if you are on your way south from Boulogne on the D901. Now sitting with a prime view over the Canache valley, its quaint streets are filled with 17th- and 18th-century houses that were built around Vauban's impressive, though now ruined, **Citadelle** (*Open: mid-Apr–*

mid-Oct daily 10am–noon & 2–6pm; Mar–mid-Apr & mid-Oct–end Nov Wed–Mon 10am–noon & 2–6pm. Admission charge). There's quite a bit to see, including two round towers dating from the 13th and 14th centuries and an 18th-century chapel, and it's possible to walk all the way around the 16th-century brick and stone ramparts.

Saint-Valéry-sur-Somme

Another tiny fishing village, Saint-Valéry distinguishes itself by being the point from where William the Conqueror set sail for England in 1066. This fact and its still-intact medieval streets have drawn visitors here for over a century – and like many places on the north coast of France, it was once popular with Impressionist painters. As well as a broad, sweeping and – when the tide races in – sometimes treacherous beach, the town has a few things worth seeking out. Most notable are: the **castle tower** where Joan of Arc was briefly held before being taken to Rouen to meet her fate; what remains of the abbey founded in 611 by the Gualaric monk Valery, with its lovely Chapelle des Marins overlooking the bay (*Rue de l'Abbaye*); and the rambling walled herb garden, the **Herbarium des Remparts** in the old hospital (*36 rue Brandt. Tel: 03 22 26 69 37. www.jardin-herbarium.fr. Open: mid-Apr–Oct Tue–Fri 10am–6pm, Sat & Sun 10am–noon & 3–6pm. Admission charge*).

Rue Saint-Jean in the heart of tourist-friendly Le Touquet

ARRAS AND THE SOMME

The area all around Arras, prosperous medieval capital of the Artois region, saw some of the most prolonged and horrific slaughter of World War I as Allied forces struggled, largely in vain, to break through the German Front. Around the town of Albert and the valley of the Somme, 30km (19 miles) south of Arras, the Battle of the Somme raged for four and a half months from July to November of 1916 and the land is now covered with poignant war cemeteries, memorials and museums (*see 'Circuit de Souvenir', pp46–7*). North of Arras, at Vimy ridge, now overlooked by an imposing white monument, you can visit the preserved trenches inhabited by the Canadian Corps for nearly two years before they took the strategically important Hill 145.

Arras

Bequeathing its name to the medieval tapestry wall hangings found throughout the castles of Europe in the Middle Ages (and behind which they found Polonius in *Hamlet*), Arras' stately Flemish and Dutch squares, town hall and belfry were sensitively restored to their 17th- and 18th-century glory following the destruction wreaked during World War I. The town is also

Arras' imposing Gothic Hôtel de Ville

The Somme's battle-scarred land serves as a poignant reminder of World War I

notable as the birthplace of French revolutionary Maximilien Robespierre, its Place du Théâtre witnessing many beheadings by guillotine.

Arras' heart is its arcaded **Grand'Place** and the bustling **Place des Héros** nearby. On the latter, stands the splendidly Gothic **Hôtel de Ville** (town hall) and **belfry**, which you can climb (*Admission charge*), completely rebuilt after the war. The town hall also has access to some extraordinary underground passageways and vaults built in the Middle Ages and used during World War I, which you can visit as part of a guided tour (*Tours arranged through the tourist office in the Hôtel de Ville. Tel: 03 21 51 26 95. www.arras.fr. Open: mid-Sept–Mar 10am–noon & 2–6pm; Apr–mid-Sept 9am–6pm, although times may vary slightly. Admission charge*).

Also dominating the centre of the town is the elegant **Abbaye Saint-Vaast**, originally founded in the 7th century, and its attached cathedral, completed in the 19th century. The classical 18th-century abbey buildings and cloisters house the town's **Musée des Beaux-Arts** (Museum of Fine Arts), which has a collection representing the town's history through medieval sculptures, 15th-century tapestries, a few Flemish Renaissance paintings and 19th-century works (*22 rue Paul Doumer. Tel: 03 21 71 26 43. Open: Wed–Mon 9.30am–noon & 2–5.30pm. Closed: 1–8 May, 1–11 Nov & public holidays. Admission charge*).

The town has another impressive and more recent attraction in the **Carrière Wellington**, a commemoration of the New Zealand miners and soldiers who built the networks of tunnels out of a disused chalk quarry underneath the town and fought in the Battle of Arras on 9 April 1917. These dank subterranean passageways, with their World War I graffiti and other surviving relics, can now be visited as part of a guided tour (*Rue Delétoille. Tel: 03 21 51 26 95. Open: daily 10am–12.30pm & 1.30–6pm. Closed: most of Jan, 28–30 Jun & 25 Dec. Admission charge*).

Albert

The rather unprepossessing and battle-scarred town of Albert is worth a visit for its **Musée Somme 1916**, which brings to life in displays and film both the horror of the war and the filthy and claustrophobic nature of existence in the trenches (*Rue Anicet Godin. Tel: 03 22 75 16 17. Open: Feb–May & Oct–mid-Dec 9am–noon & 2–6pm; Jun–Sept 9am–6pm. Closed: mid-Dec–end Jan. Admission charge*). But the town also provides a serviceable base from which to explore the numerous surrounding cemeteries and monuments to the tragedy of the war.

Péronne

Tucked away in the upper reaches of the river Somme and 25km (15½ miles) east of Albert, the old fortified town of Péronne was occupied by the

HUNDRED YEARS WAR

Not far from the horrific events around the Somme in World War I, some similarly gruesome and muddy action took place over 500 years earlier when the French and English slugged it out for control of France during the Hundred Years War. The battles of Crécy (1346) and Agincourt (1415) were both decisive and important victories for the English, thanks largely to the pioneering use of the longbow, and both battlefields can be visited. Just outside Crécy-en-Ponthieu (north on the D111 to Wadicourt) is the Moulin Edouard III, from where Edward III watched the battle rage, while 30km (19 miles) northeast on the D928 is Azincourt, where you can get a blow-by-blow account of the action as well as a detailed map of the battle lines at the Centre Historique Medieval Azincourt (*Rue Charles VI, Azincourt. Tel: 03 21 47 27 53. www.azincourt-medieval.fr. Open: Apr–Sept daily 10am–6pm (Jul & Aug to 6.30pm); Nov–Mar Wed–Mon 10am–5pm. Admission charge*).

Germans during the war and largely flattened. But it's still a pleasant, bustling place to visit and makes for a bigger and better base than Albert. Its main attraction is the **Historial de la Grande Guerre** (Museum of the Great War), an interesting war museum housed in the town's 13th-century castle and the modern Corbusier-style extension added in 1992 (*Château de Péronne. Tel: 03 22 83 14 18. www.historial.org. Open: daily 10am–6pm. Closed: mid-Dec–mid-Jan. Admission charge*). As well as some permanent exhibits illustrating what life was like for both those on the front line and civilians caught up in the fighting, and an exhibit examining the lot of prisoners held captive during the war, the museum often also has some highly regarded temporary exhibitions.

Vimy ridge

The 7km (4¼-mile)-long and 60m (197ft)-high escarpment at Vimy, 8km (5 miles) north of Arras, was of crucial strategic importance during the war and therefore the scene of protracted, entrenched fighting, both above and below ground, as the Germans tried to defend their position and the Allies sought to push them back. Success finally came, at huge cost, thanks to the Canadian Expeditionary Force in April 1917. After the war, a 100-hectare (247-acre) section of the battleground was given by the French people in perpetuity to the Canadians in recognition of their service and sacrifice and this is now site of the **Canadian National Vimy Memorial** (*Tel: 03 21 50 68 68. Open: Apr–Oct daily 10am–6pm; Nov–Mar daily 9am–5pm. Free admission*). The imposing stone-clad concrete monument, soaring over 30m (98ft) into the sky and perched on Hill 145, the highest point of the escarpment, was designed by Walter Seymour Allward and took 11 years to build, finally being unveiled by Edward VIII on 26 July 1936. It is thought that around 50,000 Canadian and French veterans and their families were there on the day. The visitor centre has an exhibition giving details of the Canadian attack and, nearby, it's possible to wander through the now-grassy, preserved trenches.

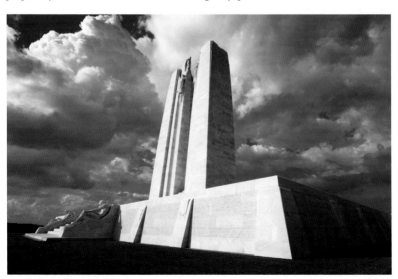

The Canadian National Vimy Memorial dominates Vimy ridge

Drive: Circuit de Souvenir (Circuit of Remembrance)

Between the towns of Albert and Péronne, there are many cemeteries and monuments to the fallen of World War I. The following circuit takes in some of the most well-known commemorative sites but you will quickly find, as you drive – or cycle – through the country lanes, that the land hereabouts is pitted with craters, still periodically spewing up an 'iron harvest' of shrapnel and unexploded ordnance.

The route is also dotted with cemeteries set peacefully in the middle of fields or just by the roadside, all with a quiet dignity of their own.

The drive covers about 40km (25 miles). Allow half a day, including stops.

Start the tour with a visit to the Musée Somme 1916 in Albert (see p44). From Albert, take the D929 northeast to La Boisselle and on entering the village follow the signs to 'La Grande Mine'.

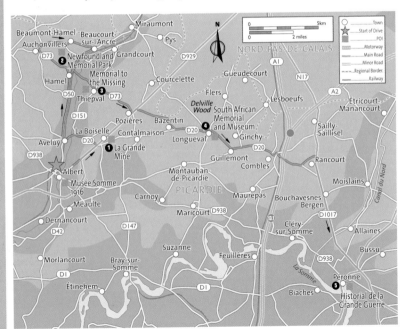

1 La Grande Mine

The Lochnagar mine crater, with a diameter of approximately 90m (295ft) and a depth of 21m (69ft), was a huge detonation exploded on the first day of the Battle of the Somme (1 July 1916). The land, which now bears a wooden cross, was bought in 1978 by Richard Dunning so that it could remain a memorial to the fighting and to the men who died here.

From La Boisselle, take the D20 west to Aveluy. Turn right on to the D50 and follow the road north to Hamel. The Newfoundland Memorial Park is on the D73 between Hamel and Auchonvillers.

2 Newfoundland Memorial Park

As well as several cemeteries in and around the village of Beaumont-Hamel, the park, bought by the Canadian government after the war, has preserved trenches that you can visit and a Memorial to the Missing, a statue of a caribou, symbol of the Newfoundland Regiment that fought here.

From Beaumont-Hamel, head southeast on the D73 to Thiepval.

3 Memorial to the Missing

At Thiepval, you will find Edwin Lutyens' striking memorial, a huge arched stone structure that can be seen well before you reach the village and whose panels are inscribed with the names of some 72,116 British and South African soldiers whose bodies were never found.

From Thiepval, head east on the D73 then the D20 to Longueval. Drive through the village. Just southeast of the village of Longueval lies Delville Wood.

4 Delville Wood

This was the scene of some particularly ferocious fighting during the Battle of the Somme. It is now the location of the **South African Memorial and Museum** not just to those who fell here but also to those who fought elsewhere in both World War I and World War II.

From Longueval, head east on the D20 to Combles and Rancourt and then south on the D1017 to Péronne.

5 Péronne

Here, you can finish off the circuit with a visit to the moving and informative **Historial de la Grande Guerre** (*see pp44–5*).

You can get back to Albert from Péronne directly on the D938, or alternatively follow the meanders of the Somme river and then take the D329 from Bray-sur-Somme.

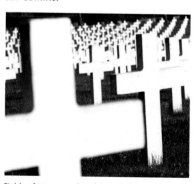

Fields of crosses: a humbling sight

Drive: Circuit de Souvenir (Circuit of Remembrance)

DOUAI TO CAMBRAI
Douai

A prosperous Flemish town, Douai grew rich on the proceeds of its textile industry in the Middle Ages and then on coal mining in the 19th century. Renowned also for its university, Douai was a haven for Catholics fleeing the persecution in Elizabethan England, and even provided them with a centre of learning in the form of the English College, a Catholic seminary that flourished here for 200 years until the French Revolution. Still an important industrial and academic hub today, despite the rapid decline in mining in the area since the 1970s, the town's wealth is most obvious in its magnificent **Hôtel de Ville (town hall)** and its (visually and aurally) spectacular belfry (*70 place d'Armes. Tel: 03 27 88 26 79. www.ville-douai.fr. Open: guided tours Jul–Aug daily 10am, 11am, 2pm, 3pm, 4pm, 5pm & 6pm; Sept–Jun daily 11am, 3pm, 4pm & 5pm. Closed: Mon morning. Admission charge*). Just off the main square, Place d'Armes, the Hôtel de Ville is a 15th-century Gothic creation and worth a visit for its guided tours of the 15th–18th-century interior rooms of governance and state (Douai was the seat of local government under Louis XIV). Next door is the at once ornate and austere 15th-century belfry with its peal of 62 bells (covering a range of five octaves). The trip up the 192 steps is more than worth the effort. The belfry is the largest in Europe and you won't have

to wait long to hear the bells ring out because they chime a different tune every quarter of an hour (as well as providing concerts at 11am every Saturday).

Across the river Scarpe and north of the centre, the **Musée de la Chartreuse** (Charterhouse Museum) is perhaps the best reason to visit Douai (*130 rue des Chartreux. Tel: 03 27 71 38 80. Open: Wed–Mon 10am–noon & 2–6pm. Closed: public holidays. Admission charge*). The old charterhouse dates from the 16th century and now houses a fabulous array of Flemish paintings from that period (look out for the work of local artist Jean Bellegambe, as well as pieces by Rubens and Jordaens), some Italian Renaissance gems (Veronese and Carracci) and some impressive later French works (by David, Renoir, Sisley and Pissarro).

Centre Historique Minier (Centre of Mining History), Lewarde

In an old disused (like most of the others in this once great coal-mining region of France) colliery outside the town of Lewarde, 7km (4¼ miles) east of Douai, the Centre of Mining History provides a fascinating insight into the work and lives of those who dug out the coal seams hundreds of metres below ground. Visits into the dark and claustrophobic pits are guided by ex-miners and show the hard and cramped conditions that they worked in right up until 1990 when the pit closed.

Fosse Delloye, Lewarde. Tel: 03 27 95 82 82. www.chm-lewarde.com. Open: Mar–mid-Nov 9am–7.30pm (last entry 5.30pm); mid-Nov–Feb Mon–Sat 1–5pm, Sun & public holidays 10am–5pm. Admission charge.

Cambrai

Another town made rich by the Flemish textile industry, Cambrai was also an important ecclesiastical centre in the early Middle Ages. However, it is perhaps most well known as the place where the first tanks were used in full-scale warfare (by the British as they breached the Hindenburg Line on

The splendid belfry of Douai's Hôtel de Ville

Must-see Matisse in the Palais Fénelon

20 November 1917 – although they were certainly not considered an unqualified success). As well as the Baroque **Église Saint-Géry**, which houses Rubens' *The Entombment*, the **Musée Municipal de Cambrai** is also worth a look for its few artistic treasures dating from Roman times to the 19th century (*15 rue de l'Épée. Tel: 03 27 82 27 90. Open: Wed–Sun 10am–noon & 2–6pm. Admission charge*).

Le Cateau-Cambrésis

This village 23km (14 miles) east of Cambrai is the birthplace of one of the 20th century's greatest painters. Henri Matisse was born here in 1869 and, after a period studying law in Paris, came back to work briefly as a court administrator before realising his artistic vocation and moving again to Paris and then south. He must have had much affection for his home town, however, because in 1952 he established a museum dedicated to his work here and bequeathed the collection to the town. Now housed in the 18th-century **Palais Fénelon**, the museum is an absolute must for Matisse fans. With 17 exhibition rooms and over 170 Matisse works, this is the third-largest collection of his work in existence. There is also a display of Henri Cartier-Bresson photographs (*Palais Fénelon, Place Commandant-Richez. Tel: 03 27 84 64 50. Open: Jun–Aug 10am–6pm; Sept–May Wed–Mon 10am–12.30pm & 2–6pm. Closed: public holidays. Admission charge*).

AMIENS TO BEAUVAIS
Amiens

Suffering considerable damage during both world wars, Amiens nevertheless boasts one of France's finest cathedrals, a masterpiece of pure Gothic uniformity, and the largest of its kind in France. In an area renowned for its spectacular ecclesiastical architecture, and following in the footsteps of Notre-Dame in Paris and Reims' Cathédrale, Amiens' Cathédrale Notre-Dame can certainly hold its head high. But this is not the only reason to visit the capital of the Picardy region: the gentrified canal streets of the quartier Saint-Leu, to the north of the cathedral quarter, hum with restaurants and bars (and a lively student population); and just north of the train station are the *hortillonnages*, bountiful medieval market gardens threaded with a canal irrigation system from the Somme and Arve rivers and producing vegetables that are still sold in the Saturday morning market.

A UNESCO World Heritage Site, the **Cathédrale Notre-Dame** soars up, dominating the centre of the city with its 42.5m (139ft)-high nave and 112m (367ft)-high spire. Its sheer size is breathtaking, but the cathedral's beauty lies in the fact that it was built in a comparatively short space of time (between 1220 and 1260) and so retains

Café culture on the banks of the Somme at Amiens' Quai Belu

a Gothic purity unmatched by many of France's other cathedrals, most of which were built over centuries rather than decades and were therefore subject to various changes in architectural style. Highlights of Amiens' masterpiece include: the restored and stunning western façade with its flamboyant 16th-century stained-glass rose window; a trip up the 307 steps of the north tower for 360-degree views of the city as well as a closer look at the cathedral's statuary; and the gorgeously crafted 16th-century choir stalls. During the summer (and over the Christmas holidays), a *son et lumière* (sound and light) show illuminates the west front brilliantly, providing descriptions of the various huge effigies, their vermilion reds, amber yellows and lapis blues vividly bringing to life the building's original polychromatic façade (*Show times: Jun 10.45pm; Jul 10.30pm; Aug 10pm; Sept 9.45pm; Dec holidays 7pm. Free admission*). Look out, too, for Viollet-le-Duc, the cathedral's 19th-century restorer, whose gargoyle-like head on the central portal is twisted round to admire his own handiwork (*Cathédrale Notre-Dame, Place Notre-Dame. Tel: 03 22 71 60 50. www.amiens-cathedrale.fr. Cathedral open: Apr–Sept 8.30am–6.30pm; Oct–Mar 8.30am–5.30pm. Choir open: daily 3.30pm. Admission charge*).

The colourful *hortillonnages*, on the outskirts of town to the east, cover an area of about 300 hectares (740 acres)

GERBEROY, LA VIE EN ROSE

On your way south from Amiens to Beauvais you may feel like making a detour to Gerberoy, about 20km (12½ miles) northwest of Beauvais. This gem of a village, officially labelled as one of the *plus beaux villages de France* (most beautiful villages in France), is especially gorgeous in late spring and early summer when the half-timbered and brick-and-flint buildings on its ancient, cobbled streets are smothered in roses.

and have been producing fruit and vegetables since the Middle Ages. Although these days it's a considerably more boutique and touristy affair than it was in the time when the gardens supplied the whole city with produce, there are still cultivators growing whole fields of vegetables in the fertile alluvial swamp. The gardens are accessible only by boat, and in summer you can take a guided trip on the traditional flat-bottomed punt-like craft from the **Maison des Hortillonnages** (*54 boulevard Beauvillé. Tel: 03 22 92 12 18. Open: Apr–Sept daily from 2pm. Admission charge*).

Fans of Jules Verne will no doubt want to visit the **Maison de Jules Verne**, where he spent the last 20 years of his life. He wrote *Around the World in Eighty Days* here, and you can see a replica of the tiny study room in which his books were written, along with various personal items and thousands of documents relating to his life in Amiens (*2 rue Charles Dubois. Tel: 03 22 45 45 75. Open: mid-Apr–mid-Oct Mon & Wed–Fri 10am–12.30pm &*

2–6.30pm, Tue 2–6.30pm, Sat & Sun 11am–6.30pm; mid-Oct–mid-Apr Mon & Wed–Fri 10am–12.30pm & 2–6pm, Sat & Sun 2–6pm. Closed: public holidays. Admission charge).

Beauvais

Yet another town rebuilt after World War II, Beauvais' main attraction is its **Cathédrale Saint-Pierre**, an aspiring Gothic creation with thwarted ambitions to upstage all others. In a wealthy medieval town ruled by bishops, the cathedral that stands at the centre of the city today was built in the 13th century and, in a direct attempt to compete with the huge cathedral at Amiens in particular, was intended to be the biggest of them all. This dream, realised briefly in the later 13th century, came to dust when the vast chancel collapsed in 1284 and was patched up with piers and flying buttresses 40 years later. Further building work on the transept, tower and spire took place in the early 16th century, only for the 153m (502ft) structure to come crashing down four years later in 1573 – ironically on Ascension Day. What you see today is an unfinished testament to the great ecclesiastical pride and overarching ambition of the Middle Ages, with no spire and no nave, but nevertheless with an esoteric beauty and powerful vaulting, which at over 48m (157ft) high still makes it the tallest cathedral in France. To the west of the transept are the remains of the original Carolingian cathedral, the Basse-Oeuvre that was built between 751 and 987, which have proved considerably more resilient than their higher-tech Gothic descendant.

Cathédrale Saint-Pierre, Rue Saint-Pierre. Tel: 03 44 48 11 60.
www.cathedrale-beauvais.fr.
Open: Jul–Aug & early Sept 9am–6pm; late Sept–Jun 9am–12.30pm & 2–6.30pm (Nov–Apr to 5.30pm).
Free admission.

Beauvais' Cathédrale Saint-Pierre is extravagant yet incomplete

COMPIÈGNE AND SURROUNDS
Compiègne

Lying just 85km (53 miles) north of Paris, the commuter town of Compiègne has one main claim to fame: its château, a splendidly restored 18th-century palace built for the French kings on the edge of the vast hunting grounds of the Forêt de Compiègne (*see pp128–30*), then later enjoyed as an out-of-town party palace by emperors Napoleon I and III. As a consequence, the town has seen its fair share of historic events, not least the signing of the Armistice of World War I at the Clarière de l'Armistice on the northern edge of the forest.

The château, called the **Palais de Compiègne**, overshadows the rest of the town, its neoclassical 18th-century exterior covering a huge area just east of the town centre. Inside, there's a vast and fascinating array of rooms, decorated in the different styles of the palace's very different residents. One moves from the elegant neoclassicism of Louis XV (who had the palace completely rebuilt) through the bedchamber of Louis XVI with its wonderful view of the park down the Avenue des Beaux-Monts to the forest beyond (he met his future wife, Marie Antoinette, here in 1770) to the considerably more brash ostentation of Napoleon I and his nephew Napoleon III. The palace also houses two museums, the **Musée du Second Empire**, with its host of flamboyant Napoleon III-era *objets*, and the **Musée de la Voiture** (guided tour only), opened in 1927 and showcasing all manner of antique locomotion, including 18th-century carriages, steam cars, bikes and trikes. Outside, the monumental garden stretching seamlessly into the forest makes for a pleasant stroll or even a picnic.
Palais de Compiègne and museums. Tel: 03 44 38 47 02. www.musee-chateau-compiegne.fr. Open: Wed–Mon 10am–6pm. Closed: public holidays. Admission charge (except on first Sun of the month).

The ancient deciduous forest itself covers 500 hectares (1,235 acres) with beech and oak, has wonderful viewpoints in the Beaux-Monts hills, and provides some great walking and cycling along its paths and hunting rides. To the north of the forest, near the river Ainse, lies the Wagon du Maréchal Foch, in the **Clarière de l'Armistice** (Clearing of the Armistice), a replica of the train carriage in which the Armistice between the Allies and the defeated Germans was signed on 11 November 1918. The original was taken away by the Nazis during World War II when Hitler, no doubt with a powerful sense of symbolic irony if not actual gloating hubris, made the French sign their own humiliating surrender on the same spot. The small museum shows some newspapers, maps, photographs and other relics from the historic events that took place here (*Tel: 03 44 85 14 18. Open: Wed–Mon 10am–6pm. Admission charge for museum only*).

Château de Pierrefonds

About 14km (9 miles) southeast of Compiègne is this fairy-tale confection of a castle, completely restored – not a little fancifully – from its 15th-century origins in the 1860s by Napoleon III's favourite architect, Viollet-le-Duc. All crenellations, drawbridges and pointed turrets, it's no surprise that the château has been used as the backdrop in many a swashbuckling epic film. For fantasists, there's plenty to see here from the sentry walks and towers overlooking the village of Pierrefonds – but it's popular with tourists so you won't be alone.

Tel: 03 44 42 72 72. Open: May–Aug daily 9.30am–6pm; Sept–Apr Tue–Sun 10am–1pm & 2–5.30pm. Closed: public holidays. Admission charge.

Laon

Former French capital during the Carolingian era and religious centre thereafter, medieval Laon sits perched on a high ridge – a useful vantage point overlooking the plains of Picardy – and enclosed in 13th-century ramparts. Its

The north

Château de Pierrefonds: with towers in which you might expect to find princesses imprisoned

Cathédrale Notre-Dame, renowned as a magnificent and beautiful example of early Gothic style, is one of the oldest in France (it was built between 1150 and 1230) and boasts five spires and a soaring nave climbing through four levels to the clerestory. Note also the rare 13th-century stained glass that lights up the Gothic interior from the rose window dedicated to the liberal arts in the north transept and at the flat eastern end (*Open: daily 9am–7pm. Free admission, and guided tours available from the tourist office on Place du Parvis. Tel: 03 23 20 28 62. www.tourisme-paysdelaon.com*).

Aside from its cathedral, the rest of Laon's medieval **Ville-Haute** (which is also accessible via a little funicular railway if you don't want to get your car stuck in the narrow medieval streets) deserves at least an hour's wander to explore its maze of ancient alleys, preserved buildings and rampart walkways.

Soissons

Another ancient capital, this time from the Merovingian period, Soissons, about 30km (19 miles) southwest of Laon, has two impressive ecclesiastical buildings to offer. Firstly, there's what remains of the **Ancienne Abbaye de Saint-Jean-des-Vignes**. Once one of France's greatest monasteries, the building suffered at the hands of the Revolution, its stone plundered to build houses in the town and repair the cathedral. The west front has been

preserved, however, and stands proud with its two Flamboyant Gothic bell towers (*Tel: 03 23 53 17 37 (tourist office). Open: Apr–Sept Mon–Fri 9am–noon & 2–6pm, Sat & Sun 2–7pm; Oct–Mar Mon–Fri 9am–noon & 2–5pm, Sat & Sun 2–6pm. Free admission*).

The **Cathédrale Saint-Gervais-et-Saint-Protais** is another fine Gothic building, if a little pockmarked from fighting in the town during World War I, and houses a treasure in Rubens' recently restored painting *The Adoration of the Shepherds* (*Place Fernand-Marquigny. Tel: 03 23 53 17 37 (tourist office). Open: Jul–Aug 9.30am–noon & 2–6.30pm; Sept–Jun 9.30am–noon & 2–4.30pm. Free admission*).

Coucy-le-Château-Auffrique

High up on a woody outcrop overlooking the Ailette valley, and about 30km (19 miles) west of Laon, sits what was once one of Europe's largest castles. Following World War I, not much remained of **Coucy-le-Château**, seat of the powerful early 13th-century lord, and at one point would-be French king, Enguerrand III. But you can still get a good idea of just how imposing this fortress was, and what a potential threat to any monarch it might have been, as its great walls and towers enclose the entire village of Coucy-le-Château-Auffrique today. The keep was destroyed by the Germans in 1917 but you can still see the foundations of a chapel and the

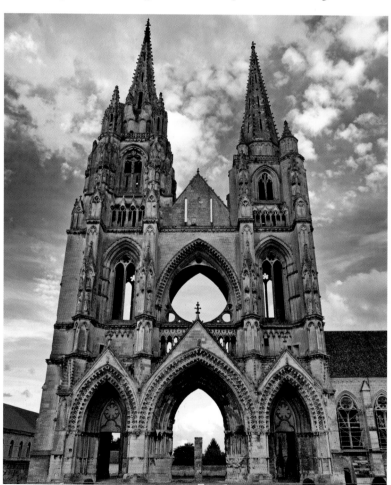

remains of two rooms and a cellar in the castle proper, as well as three original gates in the heavily fortified walls by which you enter the village. One of the gates, Porte de Soissons, has a tower built into it that houses a museum displaying some interesting photographs of the castle pre-1917. The village is a delightful place to explore (and even stay, *see 'Directory'*) for a sense of how life was lived behind these claustrophobic but protecting walls. *Coucy-le-Château. Tel: 03 23 52 71 28. Open: May–Aug 10am–1pm & 2–6.30pm; Sept–Apr 10am–1pm & 2–5.30pm. Admission charge.*

The magnificent ruins of the abbey at Soissons

Champagne-Ardenne

Champagne, a name that fizzes throughout the world with the tang of decadence and glamour, has many more strings to its bow than the mere creation of one of the world's most sought-after drinks, which, after all, really only took off in the late 18th century. The region stretches from the Belgian border to almost as far as Dijon, 350km (218 miles) further south – giving plenty of scope for variety of landscape, gastronomy and culture.

People have been growing wine in the area around Reims and Épernay since Roman times, but the region's claim to fame was once much more closely linked to Reims' soaring Gothic cathedral, home of a powerful archbishopric and scene of the coronation of 25 French kings. South of the city, the Montagne de Reims is a chalky ridge falling down to the river Marne and the heart of the Champagne Appellation d'Origine Contrôlée (AOC, 'controlled designation of origin') area. Here, you can easily spend a day visiting bustling little wine-growing villages and taking in the sweeping views of vines stretching as far as the eye can see. Further south, Troyes, former capital of the Counts of Champagne, also has a fascinating history and is a charming town to explore. At Colombey-les-Deux-Églises, you can visit the house and new memorial museum of one of France's heroes, Général Charles de Gaulle, and at Cirey-sur-Blaise in the fertile

'Champagne Humide' to the east, you can visit the home of another, one François-Marie Arouet, better known as Voltaire.

Meanwhile, if you are after unspoilt, dramatic scenery, Les Ardennes to the north with its densely wooded, hilly terrain, will not disappoint.

Leaning timber buildings in Troyes

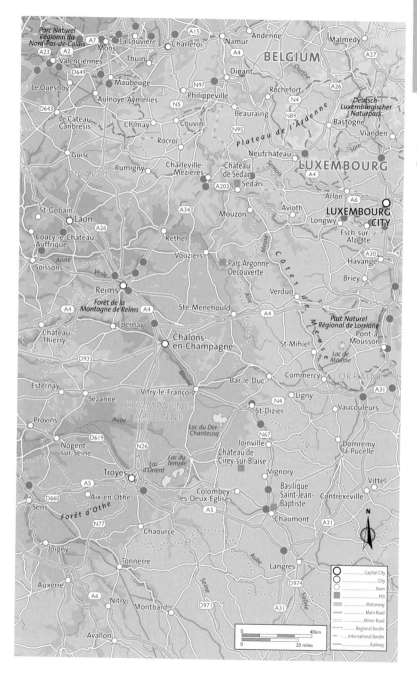

Reims

Champagne capital and for centuries witness to the coronation of French kings at its glorious cathedral, Reims occupies a special and exalted place in the French psyche. Consequently, there's a confidence – even swagger – about this city that you won't find anywhere else in this part of France. Despite the destruction wrought during World War I (many of its buildings now date from the 1920s and '30s), Reims still has an impressive clutch of grand sights dating back to the late days of the Roman Empire and, hidden away under its affluent streets, mile upon mile of chalky champagne cellars to be explored.

Basilique Saint-Remi

Named after the Bishop of Reims who christened Clovis, this ancient abbey was consecrated in the mid-11th century and is an interesting blend of Romanesque and Gothic. Its interior lends it a wonderful medieval atmosphere, which is added to by the fact that this is also the resting place of many of the early French kings and archbishops. As well as its Gothic basilica and chapels, the abbey also houses a museum in other buildings that were restored in the 17th and 18th centuries. Here, you can see artefacts from the ancient Gallo-Roman city of Durocortorum, which later became Reims, as well as Renaissance-era tapestries and artworks telling stories from the Merovingian and medieval periods.

53 rue Simon. Tel: 03 26 85 00 01. Open: Mon–Fri 2–6.30pm, Sat & Sun 2–7pm. Closed: some public holidays. Admission charge.

Cathédrale Notre-Dame

An important outpost of the Roman Empire, Reims was considered strategically crucial to the fight against the 'barbarian' hordes pushing ever further west in the final days of Rome's dominance over Europe. Following the empire's gradual conversion to Christianity, Reims' religious significance mirrored its strategic one, culminating in the baptism of the converted Frankish king, Clovis, by the Bishop of Reims on Christmas Day some time around AD 500. The cathedral that stands on this site today is the third one to have been built here. Constructed over the course of the 13th century, it is considered by many to be one of the most perfect examples of Christian architecture in existence – and certainly a fit and proper place to anoint generations of France's monarchs. The uplifting western façade is beautifully proportioned (look out for the laughing angels) and the whole building has a pleasing uniformity of style and symmetry. Inside, the narrow nave soars up through three elevations and is lit by the jewelled colours of stained glass, much of which is the work of 20th-century craftsmen (including Marc Chagall) following the damage inflicted on the building during World War I. Don't miss the tribute to

the area's wine-growing culture by Jacques Simon. It's also possible to climb over 200 steps for a closer look at the restored concrete and timber roof, as well as for views of the city.
Place du Cardinal Luçon. www.cathedrale-reims.com. Open: 7.30am–7.30pm. Mass: Mon–Sat 8am (& 7.30pm Mon, Wed & Fri). Gregorian chanting: Sun 9.30am. Admission charge to access the towers.

**Musée des Beaux-Arts
(Museum of Fine Arts)**
This museum is worth a visit for David's famous *Death of Marat* and the 27 landscapes by 19th-century French artist Jean-Baptiste-Camille Corot. There are also several Flemish Renaissance paintings along with some 20th-century works.
8 rue Chanzy. Tel: 03 26 35 36 00. Open: Wed–Mon 10am–noon & 2–6pm.

See pp64–5 for walk route

Champagne-Ardenne

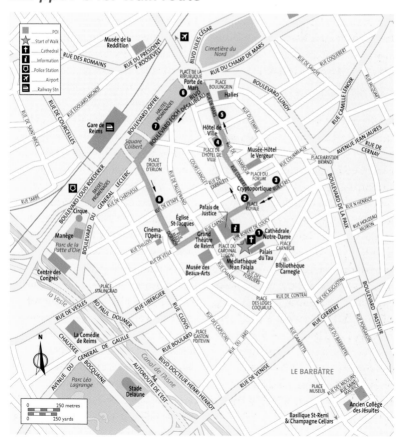

Closed: public holidays.
Admission charge.

Musée de la Reddition
(Museum of Surrender)

Eisenhower based the Allied
headquarters here at the end of World
War II. The museum has a few old
photographs and some unlikely-looking
mannequins in various uniforms, but
the map-covered room that witnessed

Chagall's vibrant stained glass brightens Reims'
cathedral

the signing by General Alfred Jodl of the
German surrender is atmospheric,
fascinating and untouched since that
day on 7 May 1945.
12 rue du Président Franklin Roosevelt.
Tel: 03 26 47 84 19. Open: Wed–Mon
10am–noon & 2–6pm. Closed: public
holidays. Admission charge.

Palais du Tau

A visit to this archbishop's palace gives
you some idea of the power wielded by
the clergy in Reims. The splendid 17th-
century building adjacent to the
cathedral was also badly damaged in
World War I but then carefully restored.
Now it houses an interesting collection
of statues that were once part of the
cathedral but which have been saved
from the ravages of the weather in
order to preserve them from decay.
It's wonderful to be able to see the
expressions on their faces close up – the
cheery angels, the grimacing gargoyles.
The sheer scale of some of the pieces is
breathtaking – Goliath is nearly 5.5m
(18ft) tall. The palace also has various
coronation treasures (it was here that
the kings stayed during the coronation
celebrations) and some wonderful
tapestries, including two 15th-century
ones from Arras that tell the story
of Clovis.
2 place du Cardinal Luçon. Tel: 03 26 47
81 79. www.palais-tau.monuments-
nationaux.fr. Open: 6 May–8 Sept
Tue–Sun 9.30am–6.30pm; 9 Sept–5 May
Tue–Sun 9.30am–12.30pm & 2–5.30pm.
Admission charge.

The Palais du Tau is a treasure trove of religious relics

Walk: Reims

For a city of such stature, the centre of Reims is remarkably small. Although a lot of it was flattened in World War I, there is much that is worth seeing, from the 3rd-century Roman Porte de Mars to the Art Nouveau and Art Deco façades built in the aftermath of the war.

Allow about an hour for this route (shown on map p61), which covers 3km (1¾ miles) – more if you plan to make stops.

Start at the western end of Reims' Cathédrale Notre-Dame.

Note: this walk takes in the main sights around the cathedral and north to the Porte de Mars. To get to the Basilique Saint-Remi and most of the champagne caves (see pp66–7), you can do a 20-minute walk southeast of the cathedral.

1 Cathédrale Notre-Dame

Facing the cathedral's main western entrance, note the myriad statues of this superb Gothic façade, some of which even appear to be laughing at you.
Turn left and walk down the northern side of the cathedral and then left again on to Rue du Trésor, past the tourist office set in an ancient ruin. Turn right on to Rue Carnot and carry on to Place Royale.

2 Place Royale

The square was laid out in the 1760s. With its arcades and balustraded roofs, it's a classic example of the architecture of the time, and one of three great squares linked together by Rue Colbert.
Cross the square and head down Rue Cérès.

3 Rue Cérès

6–12 rue Cérès is a wonderful late Art Nouveau building from the Nancy School dating from 1922.
Double back to Place Royale, then turn right down Rue Colbert. Walk up the street, over the vast Place du Forum, until you reach the Hôtel de Ville.

4 Hôtel de Ville

Reims' town hall is a rare piece of 17th-century architecture and a gem on an otherwise unremarkable square. Note the bas-relief equestrian sculpture of Louis XIII, who was king at the time of the building's foundation.
Head right past the town hall on to Rue de Mars.

5 Rue de Mars

At number 6 rue de Mars, note the mosaic panels above the 1898 Mumm

(now Jacquart) building that illustrate the champagne-making process.
Carry on down Rue de Mars to the Porte de Mars. At the end, turn left on to Boulevard Désaubeau.

6 Porte de Mars

The three-arched Porte de Mars dates from the 3rd century AD and still shows Rome's hold over this outpost of its empire in the dedication to Jupiter and depictions of Romulus and Remus, founders of the Eternal City.
Boulevard Désaubeau leads into Boulevard Foch and the Hautes and Basses promenades.

7 Hautes and Basses promenades

Laid out in the 18th century, this broad, leafy parkland area would once have seen lords and ladies in carriages parading up and down. These days, the shade generally seems to be of more benefit to the cars parked here.
Carry on until you reach Place Drouet d'Erlon on your left and turn left down the pedestrianised street.

8 Place Drouet d'Erlon

This is where Reims kicks back, the pedestrianised thoroughfare crammed with bars, cafés and restaurants. Stop for a drink at one of the many on offer (perhaps Café Leffe, *see p178*).
Continue on down the street, on to Rue Marx Dormoy and past the 14th-century Église Saint-Jacques. Then turn left on to Rue de Vesle. If you time it right, you could take in a show (or concert) at the

Grand Théâtre de Reims, its interior recently renovated in all its Art Deco glory (1 rue de Vesle. Tel: 03 26 50 03 92. www.operadereims.com).

Linger awhile at Place Drouet d'Erlon

Champagne houses in Reims

Arguably Reims' greatest 'sights' are hidden away under the city's streets – deep down in the underground chalk quarries dug around 2,000 years ago by the Romans. Taking advantage of these cool, dark, stable conditions, the great champagne houses that began to spring up in the 17th century stored their liquid, effervescent treasure here, patiently letting it mature before taking it to market.

Unlike many other great wines, champagne is a blend of different grapes – usually Pinot Noir, Pinot Meunier and Chardonnay – all grown locally in strictly classified 'Champagne' vineyards. It is this blend that gives each champagne brand is own specific quality. Dom Pérignon, cellar-master of the Abbaye d'Hautvillers in the late 17th century, was the first innovator of the *cuvée* (blend) and has taken his place in the champagne hall of fame as a result.

The champagne bubbles are produced when the wine goes through a second fermentation process after it has been bottled. Following refermentation, the sediment that is an unavoidable by-product of this process is 'disgorged' from the bottle in an intricate riddling procedure that involves manipulating the bottle so that the dead yeast sediment (lees) settles in the bottle neck which is then frozen and the icy plug forced out. At this point the sweetness of the wine is determined and the gap left in the bottle is topped up by more wine and sugar syrup before it is recorked for the last time. We have Madame Clicquot-Ponsardin (aka Veuve Clicquot – *veuve* means 'widow' in French) to thank for this refining process in the early 19th century. There are around 20 champagne houses in Reims and many more in the surrounding area, including the town of Épernay to the south (*see p70*). Each of them has brought something different – and often very special – to the drink, from the oldest, Ruinart (est. 1729), to the youngest and most precocious, such as Dosnon & Lepage set up in 2007.

A visit to at least one of the *caves* (cellars) of the great champagne makers in Reims is a must for any would-be wine connoisseur, but even for the merely casually interested the tours of these dank, cathedral-like caverns, many with beautiful bas-relief sculptures (and ancient graffiti) engraved into the chalk walls, are a fascinating insight into a way of life that has shaped Reims' identity for over 300 years. Other tours, out in the vineyards with smaller producers (such as G Tribaut, *see p69*) will give you a greater sense of the annual cycle and of the work that goes into making champagne.

The best tours will talk you through the champagne-making process (from blending the different local wines in vats, to bottling, disgorging and labelling) before showing you the vast cellars with their row upon row of bottles at various stages of maturity –

and finally offering you a taste of some of the best bubbly they have to offer. Most of the houses listed below offer different types of tour (varying in price and therefore level of detail and tasting options), so check with them first to make sure that you book the tour you want. All of them offer English-language tours.

Houses to visit
Lanson
66 rue de Courlancy. Tel: 03 26 78 50 50. www.lanson.fr. Open: Mon–Fri by appointment. Closed: Aug.
Mumm
29 rue du Champ de Mars. Tel: 03 26 49 59 69. www.mumm.com. Open: Mar–Oct daily 9–11am & 2–5pm; Nov–Feb weekdays by appointment, Sat 9–11am & 2–5pm.
Ruinart
4 rue des Crayères. Tel: 03 26 77 51 51. www.ruinart.com. Open: Mon–Fri by appointment.
Tattinger
9 place Saint-Nicaise. Tel: 03 26 85 84 33. www.taittinger.com. Open: mid-Mar–mid-Nov daily 9.30am–1pm & 2–5.30pm; mid-Nov–mid-Mar Mon–Fri 9.30am–1pm & 2–5.30pm.
Veuve Clicquot-Ponsardin
1 place des Droits de l'Homme. Tel: 03 26 89 53 90. www.veuve-clicquot.com Open: Apr–Oct Mon–Sat 10am–6pm by appointment; Nov–Mar Mon–Fri 10am–6pm by appointment.

Liquid treasure in the *caves* of Veuve Clicquot

Drive: Route de Champagne

South of Reims, the chalky slopes of the Montagne de Reims fall down to the banks of the Marne river and produce much of the top-quality 'Grand Cru' grapes that finally end up in the vats of the champagne houses. The beautiful undulating landscape is largely ancient deciduous forest broken only by vineyards stretching out from prosperous wine-growing villages. For information on caves (cellars) in each of the villages, visit www.tourisme-en-champagne.com

The drive is around 50km (31 miles), but with stops and a tasting or two could easily take a day. Follow the D980 southwest out of Reims. Turn left, signposted 'Les Mesneux'. Head through the village and continue for about 3km (1¾ miles).

1 Ville-Dommange

Fine views can be had from the 5th-century Chapelle Saint-Lié.

Leave Ville-Dommange by the road you came in on and turn right on to the D26. Follow this road for 13km (8 miles).

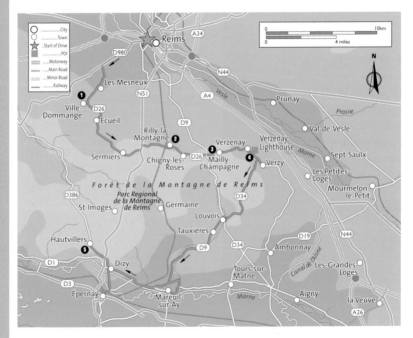

2 Rilly-la-Montagne

A visit to the Ferme des Bermont (*Route de Villers-Allerand. Tel: 03 26 97 66 50*) gives insight into the vine-growing process and its history.
Carry on along the D26 for 5.5km (3½ miles). Note the huge sculpture on your right (by Bernard Pagès in 1985) representing the Earth.

3 Mailly-Champagne

This is one of only 17 villages in the region to have Grand Cru status. On entering, you will see the modern buildings of Mailly Grand Cru, the only champagne house that uses exclusively Grand Cru grapes in all its blends (*28 rue de la Libération. Tel: 03 26 49 41 10. www.champagne-mailly.com*).
Continue east on the D26 for 3km (1¾ miles).

4 Verzenay

A lookout over a sea of vines, Verzenay's bizarre lighthouse, built in 1909, was once a somewhat racy dancehall, its flashing light attracting people all the way from Reims. These days it's part of an interesting museum devoted to winemaking (*Le Phare. Tel: 03 26 07 87 87. www.lepharede verzenay.com. Open: Tue–Fri 10am–5pm, Sat–Sun 10am–5.30pm*).
Continue 2.5km (1½ miles) towards Verzy, taking the D34 signposted to Louvois. From there, head south on the D9 to Mareuil-sur-Ay, then west on the D1 to Dizy. At Dizy, turn right on to the D386, following signs to Hautvillers.

5 Hautvillers

Like the final stop on a pilgrimage, it is here that Dom Pérignon, cellar master of the Abbaye d'Hautvillers and much-vaunted champagne pioneer, is buried. You'll find his black marble tomb in the abbey church of Saint-Sindulphe (now owned by Moët & Chandon, the house that took on his life's work). At Champagne G Tribaut in the village, you can see a smaller producer at work, visit the cellars and sample their different blends while looking out over the lovely vineyard landscape across the Marne valley to Épernay (*88 rue d'Eguisheim. Tel: 03 26 59 40 57. www.champagne.g.tribaut.com. Open: daily 9am–noon & 2–6pm. Closed: Jan–Mar Sun*).
Épernay (see p70) is just 7.5km (4½ miles) south from here on the D386.

Idyllic winegrowing countryside

Épernay and surrounds

While big-city Reims has several strings to its bow, at small-town Épernay, in the very heart of the key winegrowing areas (Montagne de Reims to the north, the Marne valley to the east, and Côte des Blancs to the south), it's really all about the champagne. If you are at all serious about your bubbly, then a stop here is an essential addition to your drive along the Route de Champagne (*see pp68–9*).

Head for the most drinkable street in the world (according to Winston Churchill): Avenue de Champagne. On the recently spruced-up strip, you will find two great champagne houses: Mercier and Moët & Chandon. Both of them offer cellar tours and tastings. At **Mercier**, there's a vast 200,000-bottle barrel to admire before being plunged 30m (98ft) underground to the 18km (11 miles) of chalk cellars, where there's an electric train to convey visitors round the galleries. Nowadays, Mercier is the biggest-selling champagne in France, a fact that would no doubt have pleased Eugène Mercier, who founded the house in 1869 with the ambition of making the drink accessible to a wider clientele (*68–70 avenue de Champagne. Tel: 03 26 51 22 22. www.champagne mercier.fr. Open: mid-Mar–mid-Nov 9.30–11.30am & 2–4.30pm. Closed: mid-Feb–mid-Mar & mid-Nov–mid-Dec Tue–Wed. Admission charge*).

Moët & Chandon, one of the biggest champagne producers in the world, as well as one of the oldest, and without a

CHAMPAGNE TERMINOLOGY

Cuvée – blend

Vintage – champagne blended from one (good) year only (e.g. 1995, 2002, 2004)

Non-vintage – a blend made from two or more different years' harvests

Magnum – larger bottle with double the capacity of a single bottle

Jeroboam – four bottles in one

Rehoboam – six bottles in one

Methuselah – eight bottles in one

Nebuchadnezzar – twenty bottles in one

doubt, most famous, has the largest cellar of all the houses on the Route de Champagne – its galleries running for a staggering 28km (17 miles). Their size is hardly surprising, though, when you consider that the company produces around 26 million bottles of fizz a year (*20 avenue de Champagne. Tel: 03 26 51 20 20. www.moet.com. Open: Apr–mid-Nov daily 9.30–11.30am & 2–4.30pm; Feb, Mar & mid-Nov–Dec Mon–Fri 9.30–11.30am & 2–4.30pm. Closed: Jan. Admission charge*).

At the **De Castellane** house, there's a museum which details all the intricacies of the champagne-making process and takes you around the bottling and labelling plant. There are cellars below ground and a 60m (197ft)-high tower that provides sweeping views out beyond Épernay to the vineyards (*63 avenue de Champagne. Tel: 03 26 51 19 19. www.castellane.com. Open: Apr–Dec daily 10am–noon & 2–6pm; rest of the year by appointment. Admission charge*).

Châlons-en-Champagne

About 35km (22 miles) east of Épernay, Châlons is an attractive, watery place. Known locally as 'Little Venice', the town is situated on the Marne river and the Mau and Nau canals, and is worth considering as a quieter, alternative base for exploring the area around Épernay. There are no sights as such, other than two impressive churches (Notre-Dame-en-Vaux and the 13th-century Cathédrale Saint-Étienne), which indicate that this quiet backwater was once a prosperous, busy place. Today, the town, with its smart 17th- and 18th-century houses overlooking canals and the river, is a pleasant place to linger.

Stroll along the peaceful river at Châlons-en-Champagne

Champagne-Ardenne

Troyes

Former capital of the Counts of Champagne and an important commercial and artistic centre in the Middle Ages, Troyes has charm in spades. Its cathedral may not have the gob-smacking majesty of Reims', and it may not be the centre of a multi-million-euro drinks industry (although it has a good number of champagne houses), but its lovely 16th- to 18th-century stone, brick and half-timbered houses, its handful of interesting churches lit up with locally made stained glass, and its attractive covered daily market give it a warmth and elegance perhaps lacking in the rival capital.

As well as wandering through the centre's cobbled streets littered with interesting civic and ecclesiastical buildings (*see pp74–5*), visitors will find a couple of museums worth visiting. The **Musée d'Art Moderne** (Modern Art Museum) houses the collection of local industrialists Pierre and Denise Lévy in a glorious 16th- to 17th-century former bishop's palace that's as much part of the display as the artworks themselves. As well as interesting and unusual 19th-century works by the likes of Degas and Seurat, the museum holds an outstanding collection of Fauvist paintings by André Derain, Georges Braque and others (*Place Saint-Pierre. Tel: 03 25 76 26 80.*

See pp74–5 for walk route

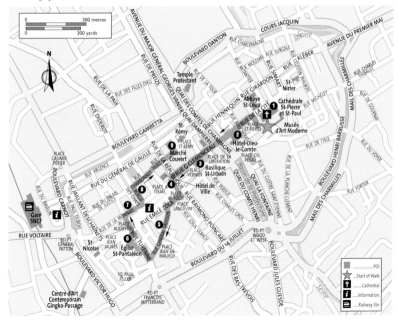

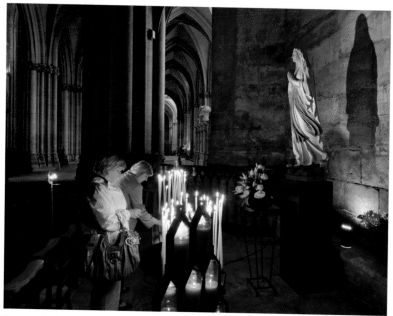

Troyes' cathedral – a place of quiet contemplation and prayer

Open: May–Sept Tue–Fri 10am–1pm & 2–7pm, Sat & Sun 11am–7pm; Oct–Apr Tue–Fri 10am–noon & 2–5pm, Sat & Sun 11am–6pm. Closed: public holidays. Admission charge).

The **Cathédrale Saint-Pierre-et-Saint-Paul** was built over several centuries from the 13th to the 17th, and although missing its second tower (which somehow they never got around to), it's an ornate joy to behold from the outside and beautifully lit up inside by various stained-glass windows, which also date from the 13th to the 17th century (*Open: Tue–Sat 9am–noon & 1–5pm, Sun 10am–noon & 2–5pm. Free admission*). Next to the cathedral is the **Abbaye Saint-Loup**, which houses

three museums in its 17th- and 18th-century buildings. You may consider giving the **Musée d'Histoire Naturelle** (Natural History Museum) a miss, but the **Musée d'Archéologie** (Archaeological Museum) has a few interesting local Gallo-Roman finds, while the **Musée des Beaux-Arts** (Museum of Fine Arts) includes some fine 17th-century Flemish masters, including Rubens and Van Dyke, as well as 18th-century French works by painters such as Antoine Watteau (*Abbaye and museums, 1 rue Chrestien-de-Troyes. Tel: 03 25 76 21 68. Open: Tue–Sun 9am–noon & 1–5pm. Closed: public holidays. Admission charge*).

Walk: Central Troyes

Troyes' central streets are framed by a champagne-cork-shaped boundary and split in two by the Canal de la Haute Seine. To the east of this waterway lies the quieter cathedral and museum district; to the west, its broader bustling streets indicate a more commercial atmosphere, although you'll pass several beautiful churches and lovely ancient town-house façades here too.

For map of route, see p72.

Allow an hour for this walk of about 3km (1¾ miles) – more if you intend to stop off at the museums on the way. Start in Place Saint-Pierre.

1 Place Saint-Pierre

Spend some time in this square admiring the lop-sided but still beautifully proportioned Flamboyant Gothic Cathédrale Saint-Pierre-et-Saint-Paul (*see p73*). To the right of it is the Musée d'Art Moderne (*see pp72–3*) and to the left is the Abbaye Saint-Loup with its fine musuems (*see p73*).
From Place Saint-Pierre, walk down Rue de la Cité to the corner with Quai des Comtes de Champagne to find the Hôtel-Dieu-le-Comte.

2 Hôtel-Dieu-le-Comte

Inside this powerful and elegant-looking 18th-century palace, you'll find a bizarre and strangely fascinating collection of medicine boxes and other paraphernalia of an apothecary's shop (*Tel: 03 25 80 98 97. Open: Tue–Sun 9am–noon & 1–5pm. Admission charge*). *Carry on over the canal and walk down Rue Georges Clemenceau to the Basilique Saint-Urbain.*

3 Basilique Saint-Urbain

Built over a very short period in the later 13th century, the basilica has a perfect Gothic unity and a profusion of utterly spectacular stained glass.
Carry on down the street to Place Alexandre Israël on your right.

4 Place Alexandre Israël

Troyes' main square is looked over by the Louis XIII-era Hôtel de Ville (town hall). Note the statue of the helmeted Minerva above the door, which replaced one of Louis XIV, and the French national motto in its original form: 'Liberté, Égalité, Fraternité, ou la Mort' ('Liberty, Equality, Fraternity, or Death').
From the square, head over Place Maréchal Foch and turn right down Rue Émile Zola, then turn left down Rue Général Saussier.

5 Rue Général Saussier

This is a wonderful street with some grand 17th- and 18th-century houses (Napoleon apparently stayed at number 11). The Hôtel de Chapelaines, at the end, has an ornate (and recently renovated so you can see all the details) façade dating from the early 16th century.

Turn into Rue Turenne and veer left on to Rue de Vauluisant and up to Église Saint-Pantaléon.

6 Église Saint-Pantaléon

This splendid church, built between the 16th and 18th centuries, has some beautiful statuary made by local Dominique Florentin, a favourite artist of François I (*Open: Tue–Sat 9.30am–12.30pm & 2–5pm, Sun 2–5.30pm*).

Head back to Rue Turenne and over Place Audiffred. Then turn right on to Rue de la Monnaie.

7 Rue de la Monnaie

This pretty street has some fine examples of 16th-century timber-framed houses.

Carry on up the street and then duck left into Ruelle des Chats.

8 Ruelle des Chats

This dark medieval alleyway has leaning half-timbered houses so close together they are almost touching. About halfway down on your left, look into the Cour du Mortier d'Or, a gorgeous courtyard and a great

example of the city's vernacular architecture.

At the end of the street, turn right on to Rue Charbonnet, which leads into Rue Huez. At Rue de la République, make for the covered market in front of you.

9 Marché couvert (covered market)

Built in the late 19th century, the market sells everything from charcuterie and cheese to fruit and vegetables (*Open: Mon–Thur 8am–12.45pm & 3.30–7pm, Fri & Sat 7am–7pm, Sun 9am–12.30pm*).

Head back to the cathedral along Rue Georges Clemenceau.

Charming half-timbered buildings line the Ruelle des Chats

East of Troyes

The eastern area of Champagne bordering on Lorraine is sometimes known as the 'Champagne Humide' (or 'Wet Champagne'). It has a fertile clay soil rather than the harsh chalky conditions found further west around Reims and Épernay, and a more rural and agricultural feel to its towns and villages.

Chaumont

Capital of the Haute-Marne *département*, the little medieval market town of Chaumont has a few attractions that make it worth a stop for an hour or so. First of all there's the **Basilique Saint-Jean-Baptiste**, unmissable with its two great towers poking out of the town's skyline. Built between the 13th and the 16th century, it's essentially Gothic in style but has a few Renaissance flourishes, work by local early 18th-century sculptor Jean-Baptiste Bouchardon, some 16th-century murals and an impressive 19th-century organ made by France's (if not the world's) greatest organ builder, Aristide Cavaillé-Coll. If you are interested in organ music, it's worth timing your visit to hear it in action. The tourist office has details (*Tel: 03 25 03 80 80*).

You can catch glimpses of the town's medieval past if you climb up to the **Donjon** (castle keep) towering over the old centre from its perfect vantage point. (There are views over the Suize valley from here.) The castle once belonged to the Counts of Champagne and now houses the town's **Musée d'Art et d'Histoire** (Art and History Museum), which includes paintings and sculptures from the 16th to the 20th century, as well as a few archaeological pieces (*Place du Palais. Tel: 03 25 03 01 99. Open: Jul–mid-Sept Wed–Mon 2.30–6.30pm; mid-Sept–Jun 2–6pm. Admission charge*).

The town's greatest architectural feat, however, is certainly its 19th-century **railway viaduct**, about 1km (just over ½ mile) to the west of the town on the D65. With 50 arches and at 600m (1,970ft) long and 52m (170ft) high, it's a remarkable achievement and has starred in several films. If you dare to walk across it, you will be rewarded with great views of the valley below.

Finally, take a look at **Les Silos**. Playing host to the annual Festival de l'Affiche (Poster Festival), this is a former 1930s grain store that's been turned into a library and graphic arts centre (*7–9 avenue Foch. Tel: 03 25 03 86 86. Open: Sept–Jun Tue, Thur & Fri 2–7pm, Wed & Sat 10am–6pm; Jul–Aug Tue–Fri 2–6.30pm, Sat 9am–1pm. Free admission*).

Château de Cirey-sur-Blaise

About 40km (25 miles) north of Chaumont in the pretty and bucolic Vallée de la Blaise is the 17th-century house that became Voltaire's home after he fled Paris following the publication of his contentious *Lettres Philosophiques* (or *Letters on the English*). Belonging to the patron, friend and lover of Voltaire, the extraordinary polymath Gabrielle Émilie de Breteuil, the Marquise du Châtelet, the house became Voltaire's home for 15 years from 1734 to 1749. While here, he carried out extensive restoration and building work on the run-down, drafty old house and added a new wing. A tour of the house is highly recommended – it's a great way to learn more about this powerful Enlightenment intellectual.

Follow signs from D2 in Cirey-sur-Blaise. Tel: 03 25 55 43 04. www.visitvoltaire. com. Open: Jul & Aug daily 2.30–7pm; May, Jun & Sept Sun & bank holidays 2.30–7pm. Tours: 2.50pm, 4pm, 5pm & 6.10pm. Admission charge.

Colombey-les-Deux-Églises

This otherwise unremarkable village deep in the heart of nowhere is forever etched on the consciousness of all French people as the home of that most truculent of French heroes Général Charles de Gaulle. He bought La Boisserie in 1934 and lived here, on and off, until his death in 1970. Though still owned by his son, Phillipe, it's possible to visit parts of this countryside retreat, where De Gaulle came to think, write and escape public attention (*Tel: 03 25 01 52 52. Open: Apr–Sept daily 10am–6.30pm; Oct–Mar Wed–Mon 10am–1pm & 2–5.30pm. Admission charge*).

As you come into the village, you'll see a memorial to de Gaulle standing on a hill just to the west of the village. It's the cross of Lorraine (symbol of the French Resistance) soaring 40m (130ft) up into the air, and below it is a new museum, the **Memorial Charles de Gaulle** (opened in 2008), complete with high-tech displays illustrating the

Brave a walk along Chaumont's viaduct for splendid views of the surrounding valley

DE GAULLE TIMELINE

1890 – Born in Lille (*see p30*)

1912 – Graduates from the elite military academy of Saint-Cyr

1912 – Joins 33rd infantry regiment of the French army

1916 – Captured and taken prisoner at the Battle of Verdun

1919–21 – Serves as instructor to Polish infantry forces and is promoted to Commandant

1939 – Now Colonel, he commands a tank regiment in the French Fifth Army

1940 – Given command of the Fourth Armoured Division and after some success at Caumont promoted to Brigadier-General

17 June 1940 – Leaves France for London following Marshal Pétain's surrender to Germany

18 June 1940 – Broadcasts famous Resistance speech rallying the Free French Forces via the BBC World Service

1943 – Moves to Algiers and becomes head of the French Committee of National Liberation

1944 – Becomes President of the Provisional Government of the French Republic

1946 – Resigns following disagreements over constitution of the Fourth Republic

1958 – Fifth French Republic formed following problems in Algeria

1959 – Elected President

1961 – Pays state visit to Germany –the first by a French leader since Napoleon – paving the way for the European Economic Community

1965 – Elected President for a second term

1968 – Following student riots and political instability, dissolves Parliament and holds new elections, winning again convincingly

1969 – Resigns following his defeat in a Senate Reform referendum and retires, aged 79, to Colombey-les-Deux-Églises

1970 – Dies of a heart attack. His will stipulates that no heads of state or ministers of the French government should attend his funeral, and he is buried in Colombey's cemetery

Langres, home of Enlightenment hero Diderot

man's life and times, from his role as leader of the Resistance through to his final days as president of the Fifth Republic of France (*Tel: 03 25 30 90 80. www.memorial-charlesdegaulle.fr. Open: May–Sept daily 9.30am–7pm; Oct–Apr Wed–Mon 10am–5.30pm. Admission charge*).

Langres

This Gallo-Roman town perched on an outcrop of the Plateau de Langres is still protected by splendidly preserved ramparts dating from the Middle Ages. You can walk all the way round the 4km (2½-mile) walls, taking in several ancient towers and gateways – as well as wonderful views over to the Vosges mountains – as you go. Inside the old town is the **Musée d'Art et d'Histoire**

(Art and History Museum). As well as some prehistoric local finds, there's a beautifully restored and light-filled Romanesque chapel dedicated to Saint Didier, a local 13th-century bishop who is reputed to have died defending the town. The story goes that having been beheaded in combat, he promptly picked up his head and walked to this spot, where he died (*Place du Centenaire. Tel: 03 25 86 86 86. Open: Wed–Mon 10am–noon & 2–6pm. Free admission*). Another local hero is Denis Diderot, a leading light of the French Enlightenment, who was educated in the town's 18th-century Jesuit college and whose presence is keenly felt all over the town in street names and statues.

Vignory

About 23km (14 miles) north of Chaumont, the picturesque little village of Vignory is rightly proud of its Romanesque **Église Saint-Étienne**. Built between 1032 and 1057, the church, which has been sensitively restored, is said to be the oldest church still in use today. It's a rare example of its kind and as well as its beautiful and austere arched, three-tier stone interior it also contains some wonderful sculpture and bas-relief stonework in the various altarpieces of its side chapels (most of which were added on about five centuries later). There's also a ruined **castle keep** (12th century) to explore at the top of the village, which makes a good place to stop for a picnic.

Champagne-Ardenne

A high-tech memorial to France's famous Resistance leader, General Charles de Gaulle

Les Ardennes

This wooded, hilly and rural little corner of France tucked away on the border with Belgium (and indeed sharing the same provincial name) is often overlooked by visitors to the region attracted by the glitz and glamour of Champagne. But, given its strategic importance on the river Meuse (which provided access, ultimately, to Paris), the area has a good sampling of historic sites, an appealing market town in *département* capital Charleville-Mézières, and swathes of unspoilt countryside to explore – whether it be by foot, cycle, car or boat (*see 'Sport and leisure', pp158–61 & 'Getting away from it all', pp131–2).*

Charleville-Mézières

As the name suggests, Charleville-Mézières is in fact two towns, but they were merged into one administrative *commune* in the mid-1960s. Each has a different feel to it: in older Mézières, to the south, you'll find late-Gothic **Notre-Dame de l'Esperance** (*10 place de la Basilique. Tel: 02 96 62 34 50. Free admission*) and traces of **medieval ramparts**; Charleville was built largely in the 17th and 18th centuries and is now the heart of the town, centring around **Place Ducale**. Often said to resemble Place des Vosges in Paris, the square is a good example of 17th-century urban planning during the reign of Louis XIII and it provided the base around which the rest of the new town was built. Its colourful

ARTHUR RIMBAUD

Born in Charleville in 1854 to respectable middle-class parents, Arthur Rimbaud was a perfect *enfant terrible* – and role model for many a 20th-century rock star. He showed signs of being a precociously talented poet from an early age and was pushed hard by his ambitious, overbearing and deeply religious mother. He excelled at the Collège de Charleville (now a library, *4 place de l'Agricuture*) and found a mentor in one of his tutors there, Georges Izambard. But pressures at home from his mother and Izambard's departure led to his running away to Paris at the age of 15. It was the beginning of a wayward, wild and globetrotting life, which ended, all too briefly, at the age of 37. But much of Rimbaud's work was written before the age of 20 and while he was at home in Charleville. *Le bateau ivre* (*The drunken boat,* 1871) was composed on what is now Quai Rimbaud, and arguably his most famous work, *Une saison en enfer* (*A season in hell,* 1873) was also written while he was back at his family home, following his passionate and destructive affair with the poet Paul Verlaine. As well as the museum dedicated to his life, you can also visit his grave at the cemetery off Avenue Charles Boutet in the town. It may not have as many visitors as Jim Morrison's grave in Père Lachaise Cemetery in Paris, but for fans (and Morrison himself was one), it's just as much of a pilgrimage site.

combination of red-brick and creamy-stone buildings and shady arcades make it a lovely place to stop for lunch. If you are interested in the history of the Ardennes, then head for the **Musée de l'Ardenne**, which provides an overview of the region through archaeological artefacts and local arts and crafts (*31 place Ducale. Tel: 03 24 32 44 60. Open: Tue–Sun 10am–noon & 2–6pm.*

Admission charge, which is also valid for the Musée Rimbaud, see below).

Just north of Place Ducale, the grand Vieux Moulin (Old Mill) on the riverside now pays homage to the town's most well-known son, Arthur Rimbaud (*see box, left*). The **Musée Rimbaud** has various memorabilia relating to the 19th-century poet and adventurer (*Quai Rimbaud. Tel: 03 24 32 44 65. Open: Tue–Sun 10am–noon & 2–6pm. Admission charge, which is also*

valid for the Musée de l'Ardenne, see above).

The town's other big claim to fame is its triennial **Festival Mondial des Théâtres de Marionnettes** (World Puppetry Festival), whose next edition is in September 2011. If you are here during this period (in which case, you must make sure that you book your accommodation well in advance), you'll get a chance to see hundreds of different shows by puppeteers from

Fresh seafood in the market at Charleville-Mézières

Archaeological and historical interest at the Musée de l'Ardenne, Charleville-Mézières

Château de Sedan

The biggest fortress in Europe, this castle with its 40m (130ft)-high wall towers over the small town of Sedan near the border with Belgium. There's been a castle here since the 11th century, but what you see here today is a slow evolution of fortifications from the 15th century onwards. Despite its size and strength, Sedan is most well known for being the scene of Napoleon III's defeat and capture in the Franco-Prussian War of 1870–71, and there's a museum documenting this as well as other aspects of the castle's history. Perhaps more exhilarating, however, are the views from the ramparts and towers. There's also a hotel (Hôtel Le Château Fort) within the ramparts (see *www.hotels-francepatrimoine.com* for further details).

Tel: 03 24 29 98 80. www.chateau-fort-sedan.fr. Open: Jul & Aug daily 10am–6pm; Sept–Mar Tue–Sun 10am–noon & 1.30–5pm; Apr–Jun daily 10am–noon & 1.30–5pm. Admission charge.

Parc Argonne Découverte (Argonne Discovery Park)

This nature park has recently introduced three wolves to one of its enclosures, which you can now visit to learn (and see) more of these fascinating but elusive creatures that once roamed this area in the wild. The hope is that two of the wolves in the small pack will breed and that there will be cubs by the summer of 2011.

around the world. If you can't time it for the festival, you can still look in at the **Institut International de la Marionette**, France's only puppetry school, which puts on student shows and other exhibitions and events (*7 place Winston Churchill. Tel: 03 24 33 72 50. www.marionnette.com. Open: Mon–Fri 9am–1pm & 2–5pm (Tue & Thur until 6pm).*

There is also another exhibition on other nocturnal creatures in the park's visitor centre (Nocturnia).

RD946 Bois de Roucy, Olizy-Primat, which is 60km (37 miles) south of Charleville-Mézières and 68km (42 miles) east of Reims. Tel: 03 24 71 07 38.

www.nocturnia.fr. Open: Apr–Jun Wed–Sun 10am–6pm; Jul & Aug daily 10am–7.30pm; Sept & Oct Sat & Sun 2–6pm; also open during school holidays & public holidays, so call or check website for specific details. Admission charge.

Champagne-Ardenne

The fountain in Charleville-Mézières' handsome Place Ducale

Luxembourg

The world's only remaining grand duchy, Luxembourg may be small but it has plenty to shout about and is worth considering as a side trip if you are in the area. A crucial strategic meeting point in northern Europe since Roman times, its capital city, nestled at the confluence of two steep, wooded river valleys, has a superb defensive – and now picturesque – location.

Outside the capital are striking hilltop castles and rolling green countryside to explore and, along the banks of the Moselle river, world-class wines to try.

Luxembourg City

A genuinely European capital now that several EU institutions are based here in the new Kirchberg part of town, Luxembourg City's position, huddled around the steep curves of the rivers Pétrusse and Alzette, has been key to the duchy's political success since the town was established in the 10th century. Once an almost impenetrable – and much sought-after – fortress, the city finally escaped overlordship by greater European powers in the mid-19th century and is now at the heart of Europe's financial and online industries.

Vieille Ville (Old Town)

Once surrounded on all sides by heavy fortifications, the small, mainly 17th- to 19th-century Vieille Ville is now more accessible since the ramparts were in part knocked down when the town was demilitarised in 1867. But what remains, on the eastern side of the Old Town, is still one of the city's most interesting and impressive sights. Head up to the **Chemin de la Corniche** and to the **Citadelle du Saint-Esprit** to get a better view. From here, you can take a lift down the side to the river valley and an area of the city known as **Grund**,

Statue of Grand Duc Guillaume II

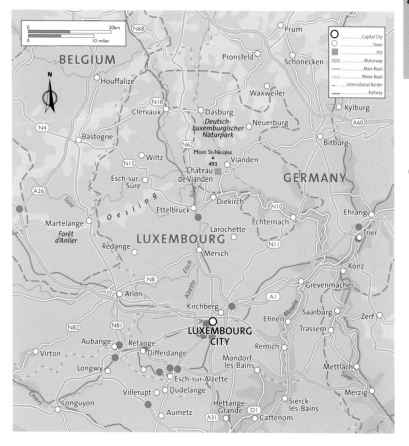

where pretty houses, once part of a working-class suburb, give way to parkland and views down the Pétrusse valley. Elsewhere in the Old Town, you can visit the excellent **Musée National d'Histoire et d'Art**, which has a particularly impressive collection of Roman artefacts, all unearthed just south of the city, as well as some decent 19th-century Impressionist paintings by the likes of Turner and Cézanne (*Marché-aux-Poissons. Tel: (+352) 47 93 30-1. www.mnha.public.lu. Open: Tue–Sun 10am–6pm (Thur until 8pm). Admission charge*). Also worth exploring is the 16th-century **Palais Grand-Ducal** (*Rue du Marché aux Herbes*), official residence of the Grand Duke, Luxembourg's head of state, which you can visit as part of a tour (*book tours in advance at the Luxembourg City Tourist Office, Place Guillaume II. Tel: (+352) 22 28 09. www.lcto.lu*).

Kirchberg

To the northeast of the Old Town, the exciting new development of Kirchberg has sprung up over the last decade. Initially attracting the finance and burgeoning online sectors, it is now home to several office blocks designed by innovative and adventurous architects (the tourist office can give you a walking map of buildings worth checking out). This is also where you'll find the part-glass and steel, part-white concrete **Musée d'Art Moderne** (MUDAM, *3 park Dräi Eechelen. Tel: (+352) 45 37 85-960. www.mudam.lu. Open: Wed–Fri 11am–8pm, Sat–Mon 11am–6pm. Admission charge*), as well as the striking white ship-like form of the **Philharmonie Luxembourg** (*1 place de l'Europe. Tel: (+352) 26 32 26-32. www.philharmonie.lu*).

Vianden's fairytale château

Moselle wine country

East of Luxembourg City, the Moselle river forms the border with Germany, and its western sloping banks provide excellent *terroir* for some good-quality white wines, especially Rieslings, Pinot Gris and Gewürztraminers. It's possible to visit wineries all the way along this stretch of the river, but **Remich**, **Ehnen** and **Grevenmacher** are probably the prettiest places to stop and the best for both wine tastings and something to eat. To get a real sense of the Moselle valley, however, take a boat trip along the river. It's possible to pick up the *Princesse Marie Astrid* boat at several points (including Remich and Grevenmacher) all the way from Schengen in the south to Wasserbillig in the north, pretty much the entire length of Luxembourg's border with Germany (*10 route du Vin, Grevenmacher. Tel: (+352) 75 82 75. www.moselle-tourist.lu*).

Echternach

About 30km (19 miles) northeast of Luxembourg, Echternach is a good base for visiting the surrounding countryside known as La Petite Suisse Luxembourgeoise, a region of jagged gorges, rivers and woods that's a popular hiking destination. The town itself is also very attractive and well worth taking some time to explore. The **Abbaye d'Echternach** and **Basilique Saint-Willibrord** were founded here in the late 7th century and, despite having been through various ups and downs

Picturesque Grund in Luxembourg's Vieille Ville (*see p85*)

over the last 1,300 years, have survived thanks to sensitive reconstruction work. Dominating the town, the complex is worth a wander and there's also a fascinating display of medieval illuminated manuscripts in the abbey museum. For more information on the surrounding countryside, visit the **tourist office** (*Syndicat d'Initiative et de Tourisme, 9–10 parvis de la Basilique. Tel: (+352) 72 02 30. www.echternach-tourist.lu*).

Château de Vianden

Teetering above a small town, about 30km (19 miles) northwest of Echternach, and surrounded by wooded hills, Château de Vianden is an impossibly picturesque must-see. There have been fortifications here since Roman times, but the Romanesque and Gothic castle you see today, almost a

stereotype of what you would expect with its rounded turrets and sturdy ramparts, was built between the 11th and 14th centuries. Unsurprisingly, the grand dukes had their eye on the place and took it over from the Counts of Vianden in the 15th century. It was an official residence until 1977, when it was handed over to the state for much-needed restoration work. You can now visit the whole complex, which contains impressive banqueting halls, vaulted galleries containing suits of armour, and a kitchen area with a cavernous well. Vianden is also a pleasant town to wander around and has plenty of hotels should you wish to stay. *Château. Tel: (+352) 83 41 081. www.castle-vianden.lu. Open: Jan, Feb, Nov & Dec 10am–4pm; Mar & Oct 10am–5pm; Apr–Sept 10am–6pm. Admission charge.*

Lorraine

Often considered something of a poor cousin to Alsace, you could be forgiven for being tempted to drive straight through this largely flat plain of not-terribly-inspiring countryside – and many people do. But there's more to Lorraine than meets the eye. As the only French region to have three borders with other countries (Belgium, Luxembourg and Germany), Lorraine saw more than its share of fighting during both world wars and has extraordinarily moving sights to visit as a result.

One of the most striking of these sights is around the city of Verdun, a name that it seems will forever be associated with the slaughter of hundreds of

Boats line the riverside at Verdun

thousands of French (and German) soldiers in 1916. But Lorraine's geographical location also makes it something of a cosmopolitan crossroads in northern Europe, a fact that ancient Metz, as proud home to the new Centre Pompidou outpost, is keen to promote. Just a few kilometres to the south, Metz's rival, Nancy, has plenty to be proud of too: as official capital of the old Duchy of Lorraine, the city's heyday came when one of its enlightened dukes set about creating an outstanding example of town planning. Further south, the Vosges mountains bordering Alsace provide plenty of beautiful scenery and outdoor activities along the Route des Crêtes, as well as pretty thermal spa resorts such as Plombières-les-Bains. And it's no coincidence that the double-barred Cross of Lorraine was used as the symbol of the Forces Françaises Libres (Free French Forces) under Charles de Gaulle during World War II: Lorraine, after all, was the birthplace of Joan of Arc.

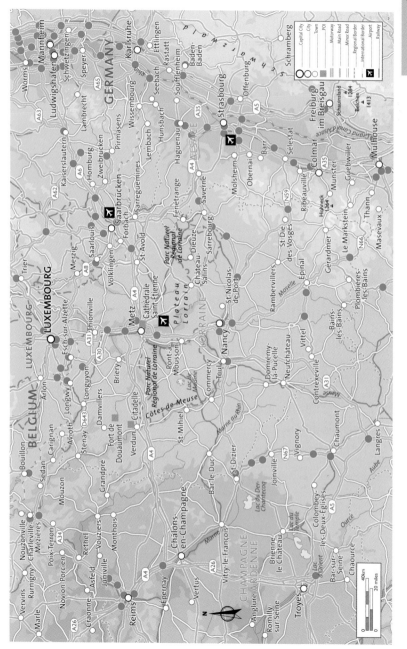

Metz

The golden-coloured city of Metz, a city once renowned – unfairly – for being a cold, industrial place with little more going for it than its status as a garrison town, has had to get a little more used to the media spotlight recently. France's latest contemporary art gallery, the Centre Pompidou-Metz (*see pp92–3*), opened here in May 2010, and Metz, which for so long hid its honey-coloured light under a bushel, has stepped on to the stage to show the world what it's made of. Aside from this spectacular new building by the station, the city also has rich architectural heritage in its medieval centre, in its 17th- and 18th-century squares – all built out of the same striking yellowy sandstone – and in its 'imperial' quarter, an area planned during the German occupation of the town (1870–1918), designed to put a German stamp on the place and encompassing a bizarre collection of various late 19th-century architectural styles as a result.

Historic centre

The heart of Metz is centred around the **Cathédrale Saint-Étienne**, which, like many of the other buildings in this part of town, is built in the sunny Jaumont stone quarried just to the northeast of the city. Built over the course of three centuries from 1220, it's an impressive Gothic building that was created out of two earlier churches (the two towers, unusually set a quarter of the way down the building from the western façade,

mark the joining point). As well as an impressively high nave, the cathedral's truly astonishing feature is its windows. Once inside, the building appears to be made almost entirely of glass. Look out especially for the Marc Chagall windows in the western transept (*Place d'Armes. Tel: 03 87 75 54 61. Open: daily*).

To the east of the cathedral lies **Place d'Armes**, a formal 18th-century square which contains the Hôtel de Ville (town hall) and tourist office and was laid out on top of an old convent. If you head north through the square and up Rue de Chanoine Collin, you arrive at Metz's cluster of museums known as the **Musée de La Cour d'Or**. As well as offering some fine art displays, this is a great place to get a sense of the town's Roman and Merovingian history, many of the exhibits, such as the remains of Roman baths, having been found during later building work (*2 rue du Haut Poirier. Tel: 03 87 20 13 20. Open: Wed–Mon 10am–6pm. Admission charge*).

Just to the south of the cathedral is the **marché couvert** (covered market) with a mouth-watering array of produce on offer – and a great place to stop for lunch or to stock up for a picnic in one of the city's parks (*Tel: 03 87 36 37 69. Open: Tue–Sat 7am–6.30pm*). The market was originally planned in 1785 to be the bishop's palace, but the French Revolution put paid to that idea and it was never properly finished. It's been the marketplace pretty much ever since.

Other squares in the old centre worth heading to for something to eat are buzzing **Place Saint-Jacques**, the strangely Italianate and medieval **Place Louis**, which, with its ancient arcades and mixture of 13th- to 15th-century buildings, was the former commercial heart of the city, and recently spruced-up **Place de Chambre** tucked in between the cathedral and the river Seille.

Île du Petit Saulcy

This little island in the middle of the river is a beautiful piece of 18th-

(*Cont. on p94*)

Exquisite stained glass in Metz's Cathédrale Saint-Étienne

Centre Pompidou-Metz

It seems a little as though an alien craft has landed in Metz. Just south of the train station, where once an amphitheatre entertained people in Roman times, you'll now find a swooping, hovering, translucent structure designed to display artwork from the vast collections of the Musée National d'Art Moderne in Paris – otherwise known as the Centre Pompidou.

It was nearly a decade ago that France's greatest contemporary art gallery decided it needed to stretch its wings and find more space to exhibit its ever-increasing collection of around 65,000 objects. Metz, something of a crossroads town in the north of Europe (it's just an hour away from Belgium, Luxembourg and Germany, and two hours from Paris thanks to the TGV) seemed to fit the bill and, crucially, was prepared to foot the bill not only for the building itself (a small matter of €70 million) but also for all costs associated with running the exhibition space thereafter. Some locals may have baulked at the vast expense but the local authorities – looking, no doubt, at what the Guggenheim Gallery in Bilbao did for that down-at-heel town's image –

saw it as a risk worth taking. And it looks as though the gamble may have paid off: within the first three months, visitor numbers to the town were up by 30 per cent and the prevailing mood in Metz seems to be an optimistic one.

The building, designed by a collaboration between Japanese architect Shigeru Ban and Parisian Jean de Gastines, is France's largest temporary exhibition space outside Paris and took nearly four years to complete. It was inaugurated by the president of France, Nicolas Sarkozy, on 12 May 2010. Essentially hexagonal in shape, the building's glass-and-steel base is capped by an extraordinary, undulating roof that gives the structure a varied height of between about 5m and 18m (16ft and 60ft). Its surface area is about 8,000m^2 (86,110ft^2) and it was made from 16km (10 miles) of glued laminated timber that intersects in hexagonal patterns said to resemble the canework pattern of a Chinese hat. Covering this wooded framework is a Teflon-coated fibreglass membrane that reflects the sun in a bright, shimmering white during the daytime but is transparent at night.

Thrust out through this in different directions are three rectangular galleries with huge sheets of glass at their ends that serve as panoramic windows focusing on different parts of the city (namely, the cathedral, the train station and the newly created Parc de la Seille in what is being called the 'amphitheatre' district).

So much for the outside. Once you have caught your breath, you can head in to the cavernous central lobby and through to four main exhibition galleries on different levels. In an interesting departure from normal art-gallery exhibition conventions, the Centre Pompidou-Metz (which is, in fact, completely independent from the Paris gallery) aims to do away with the distinction between permanent and temporary exhibitions, so that if you visit the museum once every two years, you will not see the same painting twice. It started off its first season with the spectacular *Masterpieces?*, a startling collage of some of the 20th-century's greatest art, including works by Picasso, Matisse, Miró, Giacometti, Bacon and Braque, to name but a very few.

Centre Pompidou-Metz, 1 parvis des Droits de l'Homme. Tel: 03 87 15 39 39. www.centrepompidou-metz.fr. Open: Mon & Wed 11am–6pm, Thur & Fri 11am–8pm, Sat 10am–8pm, Sun 10am–6pm. Last entry 45 minutes before closing. Closed: Tue. Admission charge.

Metz's extraordinary new cultural landmark

century architectural planning. Centring on Place de le Comédie are the **Préfecture** (Metz is now the regional capital of Lorraine), the **Théâtre** (the oldest theatre in France still being used for its original purpose, *see pp182–3*), and the **Temple Neuf de Metz**, a protestant church built during the city's annexation to Germany. Its churchyard poking out into the river provides lovely views.

Quartier Impérial Allemand

In marked contrast to the rest of the city, you will not see much Jaumont stone in this quarter that was largely planned (although not necessarily built) during the annexation period in 1870–1918. Most of the buildings are made from pink and grey sandstone, granite or basalt. Whatever the reason

for this (and some locals think that it is an exaggeration to call this area the 'German' quarter given that many of its buildings were built after the Germans had left), it's hard not the see the stamp of Prussian imperial authority in the imposing railway station built by German architect Jurgen Kröger between 1905 and 1908 (and said to have elements designed by the Kaiser himself). Opposite, equally domineering in its red sandstone, is the neo-Romanesque post office built between 1908 and 1911. In other streets around Avenue Foch, you'll find hints of Art Deco, Art Nouveau and even neo-Bavarian and Alsatian in the smart town houses. Metz has applied to UNESCO to have the whole quarter registered on its World Heritage list.

Bustling Place de Chambre next to Metz's cathedral

Nancy

Just 55km (34 miles) apart, Metz and Nancy are often lumped together as some sort of homogenous urban agglomeration by those who've never visited the two cities. Roughly similar both in size and geographical location, they nevertheless have very different histories and atmospheres, which makes for a healthy rivalry between the two cities. Whereas Metz, an important bishopric in the Middle Ages, has a certain gravitas in its cathedral and more than a hint of Prussian imperial authority in its German Quarter, Nancy, as capital of the former Duchy of Lorraine, was always the region's secular seat of power and (never annexed by Germany) benefited both culturally and intellectually from the brain-drain as refugees fled Metz after the Franco-Prussian War of 1870. With its large university, its handful of museums and its beautifully planned 18th-century streets and squares, Nancy wears its charm as a lively place of learning and commerce lightly.

Place Stanislas and surrounds

One duke in particular made his influence keenly felt in the town in the mid-18th century: Stanislas Leszczyński, former king of Poland (in exile in France) and father-in-law from 1725 to the young king Louis XV. Stanislas set about important planning work and other local reforms in the town that made him hugely popular.

Place Stanislas, an exquisite piece of 18th-century town planning, has been restored to its former dazzling glory in recent years and is undeniably the heart of Nancy – a fitting tribute to this enlightened absolutist reformer. Laid out in the 1750s, the square was designed to link the old medieval town (to the northwest) with the 'new' town built in the 17th century. Originally known as 'Place Royal' and decorated with a bronze statue of Louis XV, the square has undergone various name changes echoing the ebb and flow of French political history: following the Revolution it became 'Place du Peuple', and then later 'Place Napoleon'. A statue of Stanislas was unveiled in the centre of the square in the 1830s, with an inscription that reads 'A Stanislas le Bienfaisant, la Lorraine Reconnaissante' ('To Stanislas the Benefactor, from a grateful Lorraine'), and the place has been named after the duke ever since. As well as the Musée des Beaux-Arts on the west side (*see below*), the square's other important buildings include the Hôtel de Ville and the Préfecture on the south side and the Opéra-Theâtre to the east. To the north, the splendid triumphal arch named after Emmanuel Héré de Corny, the architect who designed the square, leads into **Place de la Carrière**. Once a place of tournaments and jousting in the 16th century, the square was remodelled by Héré and became another administrative focus of the city. At the entrance to the square are the Hôtel de

Craon (now the Appeal Court) and the Bourse de Commerce (now the Administrative Tribunal), and at the other end is the Palais du Gouvernement where the king's Royal Steward took up residence during Stanislas' time.

Running parallel to the square, the Grande Rue dates back to the Middle Ages and has a number of original 15th-, 16th- and 17th-century façades to admire. It's also home to the **Musée Lorrain**, a vast collection of over 70,000 artworks with local derivations or associations and contained in the august surroundings of the 15th-century Palais Ducale and the next-door 16th-century Église des Cordeliers. Among the works are prints by 17th-century Lorraine engravers Jacques Callot and Claude Deruet, some of which depict Place de la Carrière before its 18th-century makeover. The buildings are undergoing a long restoration programme not due to finish until 2017, but the museum remains open during this work (*64 Grande Rue. Tel: 03 83 32 18 74. Open Tue–Sun 10am–12.30pm & 2–6pm. Closed: public holidays. Admission charge*).

At the other side of Place de la Carrière is the **Parc de la Pépinière**, formal gardens also laid out in the 18th century and now the town's only large green space. Look out for the statue of 17th-century artist Claude (also known as Claude Gellée and Claude Lorrain) by Rodin.

STANISLAS' LEGACY

Stanislas Leszczyński (1677–1766), Duke of Lorraine and twice king of Poland, was an Enlightenment patron, philanthropist and even author. As well as a Collège de Médecine, he set up his own Academia Stanislaw in nearby Lunéville and is credited with making important steps towards improving the lives of the people of Lorraine. One such measure entailed providing free legal advice to those who needed it but couldn't afford it – a tradition that is still upheld on one Sunday a month in Place Stanislas to this day.

Musée des Beaux-Arts
(Museum of Fine Arts)

The city's fine arts museum was established under Napoleon in 1801 but it didn't move to its current location (in what was originally Stanislas' Collège de Médecine) until 1936. With frequent temporary exhibitions and a collection that spans the 17th to the 21st century, over three floors, the Musée des Beaux-Arts is the sort of place in which you can easily while away an entire morning or afternoon. The extension built in 1999 has provided plenty of light and space on the upper levels, where you will find works by Tintoretto, Caravaggio, Rubens, Delacroix, Monet, Modigliani, Dufy and Picasso. Excavations in the basement – an entire level devoted to Daum glassware (*see pp98–9*) – show some of the city's original fortifications. *3 place Stanislas. Tel: 03 83 85 30 72. Open: Wed–Mon 10am–6pm. Admission charge.*

Relax with a drink in front of the gilded gates of Place Stanislas

L'École de Nancy

To the southwest of the centre of Nancy (about a 30-minute walk), you'll find a fascinating little pocket of art history at the Musée de l'École de Nancy. An artistic movement born out of the city's economic, cultural and intellectual development following the migration here of many well-off refugees from Alsace and northern Lorraine at the end of the Franco-Prussian War in 1871, the École de Nancy played an important role in the Art Nouveau that was sweeping through almost all areas of design from around 1890 to 1910.

As in other parts of Europe, the artists that formed this small collective were keen to step away from an academic approach to design and art and follow a more organic – and democratic – path to beauty. They concentrated generally on the decorative arts, and their ambition was to put 'art in all' and create 'art for all'. Much of the work, from ceramics and glassware to lovingly crafted furniture, was designed in close conjunction with manufacturers, and all of the key players had workshops in Nancy producing hundreds of *objets* each year. Central to the principles of the school was the idea that method and technique were as important as design.

Émile Gallé, best known now for his glassware, was a driving force behind the movement and was head of the school. He took over his father's business selling glass and ceramics and brought in his own designs inspired by local flora and Oriental art. **Victor Prouvé** (whose haunting, Realist paintings you can see in both the Musée des Beaux-Arts in Nancy and at the Centre Pompidou in Metz) was a painter and sculptor who worked closely with Gallé, producing designs for ceramics, glassware and marquetry on furniture. **Louis Majorelle** was another craftsman who took over his father's business (this time cabinet-making) and introduced a similar curvilinear, nature-inspired style into his designs for both furniture and lamps. The **Daum** brothers (Auguste and Antonin) likewise took over their father's glass studio in the city and provided Gallé with some fierce competition.

Today, the only one of these workshops that is still in business is the Daum factory (*www.daum.fr*), and the Art Nouveau movement faded almost as quickly as it rose – certainly by the outbreak of World War I. But you can still see a whole wealth of beautiful examples of what it produced at the **Musée de l'École de Nancy**, originally the house of one of the movement's wealthy benefactors, **Eugène Corbin**. Set out much like a private house rather than a museum – you walk through drawing rooms, dining rooms and bedrooms – Corbin donated a large collection of works to the town and in 1952 Nancy City Council bought Corbin's house. The museum finally opened in 1964 and has subsequently acquired many other important Art Nouveau pieces. Look out especially for Gallé's equivocal and disturbingly decorated bed, *Aube et Crépuscule*

(*Dawn and Twilight*), designed, perhaps rather unfortunately given its rather gloomy outlook on life, for a newly wed couple, and Prouvé's equally ambiguous bronze sculpture, *La Nuit* (*The Night*). You can also explore the garden, beautifully restored, to find not only the Japanese-influenced aquarium and an extraordinarily ornate mausoleum designed by Paris architect Girard and sculptor Pierre Roche, but also many of the plants that inspired the designs you'll see on the furniture, ceramics and glassware within the museum.

36–38 rue du Sergent Blandan. Tel: 03 83 40 14 86. www.ecole-de-nancy.com. Open: Wed–Sun 10am–6pm. Admission charge.

Cabinet-maker Eugène Vallin's unique dining room, created for Charles Masson

Verdun and surrounds

A frontier town since 843 when the Treaty of Verdun divided up Charlemagne's empire between his three surviving grandsons, Verdun's position as a key strategic French stronghold sealed its fate during World War I. In the conflict that lasted 300 days from February to December 1916 and saw the Germans come within 5km (3 miles) of the town but never finally take it, the French held on to Verdun at the cost of what is estimated to be over 300,000 lives (French and German) and the almost complete destruction of the ancient town. Not surprisingly, much of what there is to see in and around the town centres on the events of this horrific conflict, but for all that, Verdun also makes a good and friendly base from which to explore the area.

Citadelle

To the west of the centre of Verdun lies the citadel, built by Louis XIV's military adviser Vauban in the late 17th century. During World War I, it was used as a fortified shelter away from the front line just to the east of the town. You can now visit and see the dank conditions in which around 2,000 men at any given time were housed before being sent to fight. There's a guided tour around the 7km (4¼ miles) of underground tunnels and galleries that re-creates scenes to give some idea of what life was like here during the war. *Avenue 5ème R A P. Tel: 03 29 83 44 28. Open: Apr–Jun & Sept 9am–6pm; Jul &* *Aug 9am–7pm; Mar, Oct & Nov 9.30am– 5.30pm; Feb & Dec 10am–noon & 2–5pm. Closed: Jan. Admission charge.*

Monuments to the war

Verdun has many monuments to the conflict that provide a moving framework for the rebuilt town. Not far from the train station (opposite Porte Saint-Paul) is Rondin's bronze of a frustrated Victory trying to take flight but being pulled back down to the ground by the body of a soldier. At the end of Avenue de le Victoire on Place de le Libération is the Monument de la Victoire, a towering structure with 73 steps leading up to a plinth on which stands a stone statue of a stalwart soldier leaning on his sword. Over the Meuse river, at Place de le Nation, stands a third memorial to the fallen, this time depicting five men, each representing different parts of the French forces, standing together seemingly forming an impenetrable wall of defence.

Verdun's battlefield

Visiting the battlefield surrounding Verdun is a sobering experience. The land, pock-marked and pitted with shell craters and trenches, is part of the 'zone rouge', an area still off-limits to development because of the devastation wrought during the war and the still-present danger of unexploded ordnance. Nine villages (Beaumont, Bezonvaux, Cumières, Douaumont, Fleury-devant-Douaumont, Haumont-près-

Samogneux, Louvemont-Côte du Poivre, Ornes and Vaux-devant-Damloup) were completely wiped off the map during the fighting and, because of the 'zone rouge' status, were never rebuilt. As well as the small memorials erected where these villages once were, there are forts at Douaumont (*see below*) and Vaux that you can visit, a memorial museum at Fleury (*see below*) and the ossuary at Douaumont (*see below*) that has come over the last 60 years to symbolise peace and unity between France and Germany.

Set on the highest ground of the immediate area and dug into the hillside, the **Fort de Douaumont**, about 13km (8 miles) northeast of Verdun by road, was the strongest defence that Verdun had, but it was nevertheless

Rodin's statue commemorates Verdun's hideous so-called victory

The Ossuaire Douaumont stands as a dreadful reminder of the loss of human life

taken easily by the Germans in the spring of 1916. It then took the French eight months of constant bombardment to recapture it. A visit here is worthwhile to get a sense of the conditions that the Germans suffered during the campaign. The fetid, clammy quarters lacked enough oxygen, let alone running water or any form of heating, for the 3,000 men camped here. As well as a gun turret and barrack rooms, there is also a memorial to the 679 Gemans interred here as the fighting raged around them (*Tel: 03 29 84 41 91. Open: Feb, Mar, Nov & Dec 10am–5pm; Apr & Sept 10am–6pm; May–Aug 10am–6.30pm. English audio guide available at the desk. Admission charge*).

Just up the road from the fort stands the **Ossuaire Douaumont** (Douaumont Ossuary), France's largest memorial to the fallen of World War I. Containing the remains of over 130,000 unidentified combatants (both French and German) from the Battle of Verdun, the ossuary is split into different chambers that represent the different sectors of the battlefield. You can see the human bones through small windows into these rooms from the outside of the building. In the middle of the monument is a 46m (151ft)-high tower, the Tour des Morts, which was designed to represent one of the thousands of shells fired during the battle. Inside, the walls and ceiling of the building are lined with the names and dates of missing soldiers, some just 18 years old. Remains of corpses are still occasionally found on the battlefield and, when they are, they are brought here to be interred (*Open: mid–end Feb & Dec 2–5pm; Mar & Nov 9am–noon & 2–5pm; Apr–Aug 9am–6pm; Sept 9am–noon & 2–6pm; Oct 9am–noon & 2–5.30pm. Closed: Jan–mid-Feb. Free admission*).

In another of the destroyed villages, Fleury-devant-Douaumont (which was captured and regained no fewer than 16 times), is the **Mémorial de Verdun**, a memorial museum that was inaugurated in 1967. Its collection has been amassed thanks to the donations of veterans and their families, and includes displays of equipment along with photographs and film footage of the area and the battle (*1 avenue du Corps Européen, Fleury-devant-Douaumont. Tel: 03 29 84 35 34. www.memorial-de-verdun.fr. Open: Feb–Mar & mid-Nov–mid-Dec 9am–noon & 2–6pm; Apr–mid-Nov 9am–6pm. Closed: mid-Dec–end Jan. Admission charge*).

Saint-Mihiel

About 35km (22 miles) south of Verdun lies the small town that built up around the abbey of Saint-Mihiel. Occupied by the Germans during the war, it escaped a lot of the damage that was inflicted upon Verdun and other areas caught up in the conflict. It makes a decent alternative base to Verdun and it's certainly worth a stop for fans of

Renaissance sculptor Ligier Richier, who was born and lived here. **Église Saint-Étienne** has his masterpiece *Sépulcre* carving and in **Église Saint-Michel** you can see the *Pâmoison de la Vierge* (the Virgin fainting, supported by St John). There's also the intriguing **Musée d'Art Sacré** (Museum of Sacred Art) with examples of religious art from the local region as well as the rest of France (and which also includes some modern work), and a beautiful library, the **Bibliothèque Bénédictine**, both housed within the former abbey (*Rue de Palais de Justice. Tel: 03 29 89 06 47. Open: Jun–Sept Wed–Mon 2–6pm; Oct–May Sat & Sun 2–6pm. Admission charge*).

Artillery impresses at Fleury's memorial museum

Spa resorts

To the west of the Vosges mountains bordering the Alsace region, the land broadens out into a massif, or plateau, of pretty, rolling and unspoilt countryside, and here you will find several mineral-rich thermal springs. The area is renowned for its spa health and well-being tourism and, unsurprisingly, has been exploiting this natural resource since Roman times.

First of all, there's the household name of **Vittel**. Something of a pilgrimage destination for ailing rheumatics and arthritics from all over Europe in the 19th century, the town may seem a little faded now but you can catch more than a glimpse of its former grandeur in its belle-époque Grand Hôtel, spa complex and 700 hectares (1,730 acres) of parkland and forest. The Vittel Thermal Spa offers treatment with its calcium- and magnesium-rich mineral water for everything from urinary complaints to migraines, as well as providing hammams, saunas and a beauty centre. Many people come for a two- or three-week treatment, but it's also possible to visit for a single day (*Tel: 03 29 05 20 84. www.thermes-vittel.com. Open: usually Mon–Sat 7.30am–12.30pm & 2.30–5pm, but check website for more details. Reservations essential*).

Nearby, **Contrexéville**, with its turn-of-the-20th-century neo-Byzantine spa, offers a similar experience. Its five mineral springs are said to have diuretic qualities and are therefore thought to be useful as a slimming aid and for kidney and liver complaints. Again, you can also visit for pure relaxation purposes and luxuriate in its pool, sauna and hammam, and there are also other beauty treatments on offer (*Tel: 03 29 08 03 24. www.contrexetmoi.fr. Open: Apr–Oct Mon–Sat 7.30am–12.30pm & 2–6pm,*

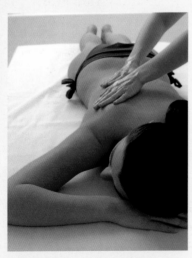

Ultimate relaxation at Bains-les-Bains

Plombières-les-Bains

of architectural styles in the town, from the Étuve Romaine (Roman steam room), which, when built in 1856, uncovered one of the original Roman baths (you can visit by guided tour, bookable through the tourist office. *Tel: 03 29 66 01 30*) to Stanislas' wrought-iron-clad neoclassical Maison des Arcades and the Bain National with its restored 19th-century façade (*Thermal Spa. Tel: 03 29 30 07 00. www.plombieres-les-bains.com. Open: Apr–Nov Mon–Fri 9am–noon & 2–5pm. Reservations essential*).

Sun 9am–noon & 4–7pm. Reservations essential).

About 65km (40 miles) to the southeast, tucked away in the wooded foothills of the Vosges, lovely **Plombières-les-Bains** has a long history as a spa resort. The Romans built baths using the hot springs here and by the 16th century the town was attracting the great and the good. The likes of Montaigne and Voltaire swore by the place and it was even good enough for Louis XV's daughters and Napoleon's Joséphine. Stanislas, Duke of Lorraine (*see p96*), also visited and has had a bath, a street and a fountain named after him, and the town was given a face-lift by another admirer, Napoleon III, in the mid-19th century. Not surprisingly, there's an interesting mix

Finally, **Bains-les-Bains**, 20km (12½ miles) west of Plombières-les-Bains, is another Roman spa town in a wooded valley. Following excavations in the 18th century, many ancient artefacts and foundations were uncovered from the Gallo-Roman era which can still be seen today. The spa's 11 springs, varying in temperature from 25°C to 51°C (77°F to 124°F), are used in the treatment of cardiac conditions such as high blood pressure and circulatory problems (*Chaîne Thermale du Soleil, 1 avenue du Docteur Mathieu. Tel: 03 29 36 32 04. Open: Apr–Nov Mon 6am–noon & 2–5pm, Tue–Fri 8am–noon & 2–5pm, Sat 8am–noon. Reservations essential*). Check the tourist office website (*www.ot-bains-les-bains.com*) for further spa details.

Drive: Route des Crêtes

This 'road of crests' was built during World War I by the French army as a supply line through the Vosges mountains, which form a natural border between Lorraine and Alsace. It's a lovely route through some spectacular scenery and well worth the detour if you are heading over to Colmar (see pp122–3). Bear in mind, however, that you will need cross-country skis (see p160) rather than a car for much of this route if you want to do it in winter!

Allow half a day for the 70km (43-mile) drive, including a few stops. Allow a day if you want to get out and go up into the mountains on a chairlift.

Start in the town of Fraize, 50km (31 miles) east of Épinal, and follow the N415 to the Col du Bonhomme.

Spectacular views across the Vosges

1 Col du Bonhomme

As you climb up the winding road you enter the forêt communale de Fraize, a dense deciduous and evergreen woodland interspersed with tranquil cattle-grazing pastures. The Col du Bonhomme, at an altitude of 949m (3,113ft), is right on the regional border of Alsace and Lorraine.
Follow signs for the D148 heading south to Lac Blanc.

2 Col de Louchbach

The D148 keeps winding upwards over the Col de Louchbach with impressive views to the south and the Meurthe valley.
Carry on along the D148 past the Grazon de Faing hill to Lac Blanc.

3 Lac Blanc

At 1,054m (3,458ft), this village is named after the glacial lake below it. There are lovely views of the lake from the little ski station here and you can also take chairlifts higher up into the mountains in summertime, for a pleasant break. If you actually want to get down to the lake, follow the D48.II.

Carry on south on the D148, which becomes the D61, signposted to Col de la Schlucht.

4 Col de la Schlucht

Another ski resort that's also open in summer. You can take a chairlift from here up to the top of the nearest summit, Montabey.

Just outside the village on your right is the Jardin d'Altitude du Haut-Chitelet.

5 Jardin d'Altitude du Haut-Chitelet

This high-altitude garden consists of 11 hectares (27 acres) sheltering some interesting, almost alien-looking, high-altitude plants and beautifully delicate wild flowers (*Tel: 03 29 63 31 46. Open: Jun 10am–noon & 4–6pm; Jul & Aug 10am–6pm; Sept 10am–noon & 2–5.30pm. Admission charge*).

Take the D430 south, signposted 'Route des Crêtes' and 'Le Markstein'. The next summit on the route is the Hohneck.

6 Hohneck

At 1,364m (4,475ft), this is one of the highest mountains in Lorraine and provides stunning views across the Vosges to the Grand Ballon.

Continue on the D430, following signs for Le Markstein and entering the Alsace region, then in Le Markstein take the D431 signposted to the Grand Ballon.

7 Col du Grand Ballon

At 1,424m (4,672ft), this is the highest point in the mountain range you can get to by car. The views are, of course, superb from up here and, coming down the other side, the Rhine valley stretches out before you to the Black Forest beyond.

Follow the D431 to Uffholtz and then take the main D83 road to Colmar.

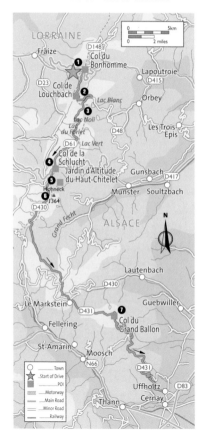

Alsace

Sandwiched between the Rhine river to the east and the Vosges mountains to the west, Alsace feels different. Neither French nor German, the region has an independent streak that is understandable when you consider its history. It only became part of France during the 17th century, was forcibly annexed to Germany in 1871, and then returned to France at the end of World War I. It was subsequently annexed again by Germany during World War II.

All this pushing and pulling by two overbearing neighbours determined to force a more homogenous identity on the region (use of the French language was banned during the German occupation, and German was outlawed when France took Alsace back again) served only to encourage a determined digging-in of heels among the Alsatians (it's politically the most conservative region of France, and many of the inhabitants still speak Alsatian to this day). This somewhat ambiguous political view of the nation state (the region was one of the few French regions that voted 'yes' to the European Constitution in 2005), and Alsace's geographical location between France and Germany, has served the region well in recent years since its main city, Strasbourg, became a European capital. The great 'crossroads of Europe' has thrived under the spotlight and is now a political, cultural and academic centre, if not exactly to rival Paris, then at least to give it a sense of competition. Running from north to south along the border with Lorraine, the Vosges mountains provide endless opportunities for outdoor activities or for simply exploring the many castles, abbeys, lakes and stunning mountain peaks by car. And, further down, the wine route which hugs the lower slopes gives a sense of the region's history and current prosperity as a string of well-turned-out and preserved wine-producing towns and villages welcome visitors to their cellars.

Pretty Alsatian architecture

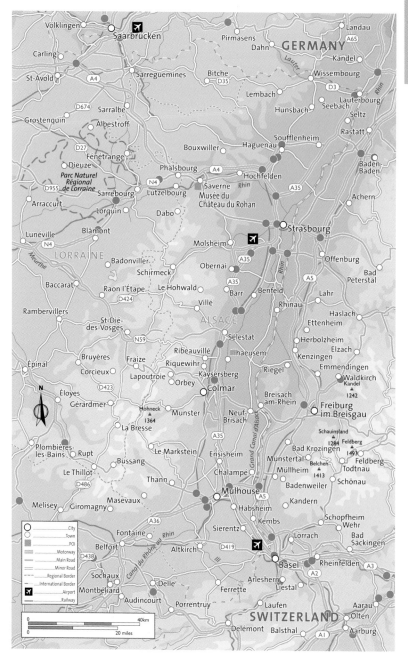

Alsace

Strasbourg

Nearer to Milan, Frankfurt, Zurich and Brussels than it is to Paris, Strasbourg, the 'city of the roads' as its Roman name (Strateburgum) meant, is big and bold enough to have a European identity all of its own. It's a character partly formed by its position as regional capital of Alsace, but also by its ancient role as one of the major crossroads of Europe, and now also by its more official responsibility as one of the three capitals of the European Union. The city also has a thriving intellectual and academic heritage, and its university is considered one of the best in France.

The city centre, set on an island in the river Ill that runs through the city, has plenty of Alsatian medieval charm in its crooked cobbled streets and hidden courtyards surrounded by half-timbered buildings. Further out, the Quartier Impérial Allemand and the new European Government area to the northeast have grand, tree-lined avenues and a more business-like feel to them.

Cathédrale Notre-Dame

Unlike Metz's yellowy Jaumont sandstone or Reims' recently cleaned creamy colour, Strasbourg's cathedral was built from the local rose-pink stone that you will see in the Vosges mountains to the southwest. It's a spectacular Gothic building, with a

See pp114–15 for tour route

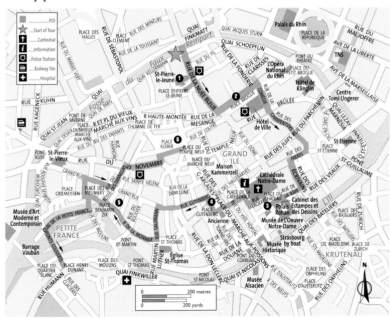

Examples of present-day imagination at the Musée d'Art Moderne et Contemporain, Strasbourg

spire 142m (465ft) high, which held the record for being the world's tallest building until 1874, but its 12th-century origins are Romanesque (an influence you can still see in the emphasis placed on walls rather than windows in the choir and south portal). The Gothic influence came in 1225 when a new team of architects from Chartres were called in and remodelled the building along its present Gothic lines. Highlights of the building include its vertigo-inducing (even from the ground if you look up!) octagonal-based spire, the 66m (216ft)-high viewing platform that links the two towers, and the technical and artistic masterpiece that is the *horloge astronomique* (astronomical clock) originally built in 1550 and 1574 and refurbished in the mid-19th century.

The clock strikes 12 at 12.30pm every day and is followed by a procession of Apostles bowing before Jesus at the top of the clock.

Place de la Cathédrale. www.cathedrale-strasbourg.fr. Open: daily 7–11.20am & 12.35–7pm. Viewing platform open: Oct–Mar 10am–5.15pm; Apr–Sept 9am–7.15pm. Admission charge. Astronomical clock tickets are available from the cashier at the south doorway.

**Musée d'Art Moderne et Contemporain
(Museum of Contemporary Art)**
This steel and glass purpose-built gallery sits in a pretty location overlooking the river and Petite France (*see p115*) beyond. The light-filled rooms display a collection that encompasses the period from 1870 to

the present day. So, along with Monet and Gauguin, you will also see cutting-edge new conceptual pieces and a lot in between. Some of the most interesting – and less well-known – work is that of (Hans) Jean Arp, a Strasbourgian and notable member of the Dada movement.

1 place Hans Jean Arp. Tel. 03 88 23 31 31. Open: Tue, Wed & Fri noon–7pm, Thur noon–9pm, Sat & Sun 10am–6pm. Admission charge.

Musée de l'Oeuvre Notre-Dame (Museum of Notre-Dame Works)

Next door to the cathedral, this museum gives you an opportunity to

BOAT TRIPS IN STRASBOURG

You can circumnavigate Strasbourg's central Grande Île (Grand Island) by boat. It's a great way to get a different perspective on the old city and you also get to see the new quarter housing all the European institutions.
Embarkation from the Palais Rohan. Tel: 03 88 84 13 13. www.batorama.fr. Boats run: Apr–Oct every half hour 9.30am–9pm; May–Sept additional departures at 9.30pm & 10.30pm; Dec every half hour 9.30am–6pm; rest of the year 10.30am, 1pm, 2.30pm & 4pm. Admission charge.

see close up some of the beautiful craftsmanship that went into the creation of the cathedral's ornate exterior as well as many other medieval and Renaissance sculptures and paintings. Housed in a building almost as old as the cathedral itself (part of a 13th-century plan to drive forward and fund raise for the cathedral-building project), the Musée de l'Oeuvre Notre-Dame's highlights include sculptures that were originally placed on the western façade of the cathedral (now replaced by copies) and the precious 11th-century stained-glass Wissembourg Christ.

3 place du Château. Tel: 03 88 52 50 00. Open: Tue–Fri noon–6pm, Sat & Sun 10am–6pm. Admission charge.

Palais Rohan

This former bishop's palace is a splendid Baroque creation built from 1731 to 1742. These days, it's home to three important civic museums. The **Musée des Arts Décoratifs** is housed in

Strasbourg's cityscape from atop its cathedral

Strasbourg is charming and vibrant by night

the sumptuous Grands Appartements on the ground floor of the palace. It has an important collection of faience and porcelain from Alsace as well as silver- and goldware and parts of the original astronomical clock from the city's cathedral, including the crowing cock that signified Peter's betrayal of Christ. It is said to be the world's oldest automaton. In the other museums, the **Musée des Beaux-Arts** and the **Musée Archéologique**, you will find works by Dutch and Italian Renaissance old masters, including some Rubens, Van Dyke and Botticelli, and local archaeological finds from the Roman and Merovingian eras.

2 place du Château. Tel: 03 88 52 50 08. www.musees-strasbourg.org. Open: Mon & Wed–Fri noon–6pm, Sat & Sun 10am–6pm. Admission charge covers entry to all three museums.

Cycle tour: Central Strasbourg

Unlike other French towns – and a lot more like German ones – Strasbourg is a very cycle-friendly city. With a comprehensive network of well-labelled cycle lanes, it's possible and highly enjoyable to see a lot of the city by bike. You can pick one up either at the train station (4 rue de Mayor Kuss. Tel: 03 88 23 56 75) or just south of the Grande Île (10 rue des Bouchers. Tel: 03 88 24 05 61).

For map of route, see p110.

Allow two hours for this route, which covers about 3km (1¾ miles).

Start at Pont du Faubourg-de-Pierre and head over the bridge up Rue de la Nuée Bleue. Turn right on to Place Saint-Pierre-le-Jeune.

1 Place Saint-Pierre-le-Jeune
The Gothic church of Saint-Pierre-le-Jeune has been on this site since the 13th century, but there are remnants of an earlier Romanesque building in its peaceful colonnaded cloister.
Back on Rue de la Nuée Bleue, carry on and then turn left on to Place Broglie.

2 Place Broglie
An elegant, tree-lined promenade-square, Place Broglie is surrounded by grand 18th-century houses, including the Hôtel de Ville and the military governor's mansion. At number 3, Rouget de Lisle, composer of the Marseillaise, performed the song for the first time for the Mayor of Strasbourg.
Turn right on to the Rue de la Comédie

and carry straight on before turning right again on to Rue des Frères, left on to Rue des Écrivains, and then right at Rue de la Râpe to reach Place du Château.

3 Place du Château
In front of you to your left is the back of Palais Rohan (*see pp112–13*) and straight ahead the Place du Château. To your right is the south side of the cathedral and the lovely clock doorway, the cathedral's oldest. The figure between the two doors is Solomon.
From the western façade of the cathedral, head directly down Rue Mercière (note you need to get off your bike at this point because there is no cycle path) to Place Gutenberg.

4 Place Gutenberg
This is one of the city's oldest squares and is named after Johannes Gutenberg who lived and worked on his printing press here around 1430–44. There's a statue of him in the middle of the square.

From the square, head west along Rue Gutenberg and then along Grand'Rue, turning left on to Rue Salzmann and then right on to Rue de la Monnaie, where you'll find yourself in the part of the city known as Petite France.

5 Petite France

This area was the former tanners' and fishermen's district – and probably smelled considerably less pleasant than it does today. Now it's a riot of colourful buildings bedecked with window boxes that are reflected in the water of the surrounding canals. At the end of Quai de la Petite France are the *ponts couverts*, covered bridges that are no longer covered as they were in the Middle Ages but nevertheless provide a good vantage point from which to view Vauban's dam, built to protect the city from floods in the 17th century.

Head back to Grand'Rue, turn right and then left on to Rue du Fosse des Tanneurs. Then turn right on to Rue du 22 Novembre and walk up to Place Kléber.

6 Place Kléber

This square, the heart of the old city, is also one of the main locations for Strasbourg's Christkindelsmärik (Christmas market). It's the biggest of its kind in France and has been held here since 1570. There's a statue of the square's namesake, Jean-Baptiste Kléber, a commoner who rose through the ranks of the army during the French Revolution to become Commander of the French Forces under Napoleon.

To get back to your starting point, from Place Kléber, head north along Rue des Grandes Arcades, which becomes Petite Rue de l'Église, then head right towards Place St-Pierre-le-Jeune and left on to Rue de la Nuée Bleue.

Place Gutenberg in the historic heart of the city

Cycle tour: Central Strasbourg

Northern Vosges

The area to the north and west of Strasbourg encompasses some lovely unspoilt countryside in the northern stretch of the Vosges mountains. The Parc Naturel Régional des Vosges du Nord is especially popular with hikers and offers all sorts of outdoor pursuits (*see pp134–5*). To the west, at Saverne on the Marne–Rhine canal, you'll find more evidence of the Rohan ecclesiastical dynasty at the elegant château they built while exiled from Strasbourg during the Reformation and, just outside, the picturesque ruin of Château du Haut-Barr. Wissembourg, to the north and right on the border with Germany, is a very pretty little town with a Teutonic twang in its local accent and half-timbered houses festooned with colourful window boxes. Further east, the land flattens out into

Musée du Château du Rohan, Saverne

TAKE THE BOAT TO GERMANY

Across the broad, swirling river Rhine lies Germany, nowadays accessible by many bridges along its length. Before many of the little bridges were built, however, people used to take their cars across on small ferries known as *bacs*. Most of these have been put out of business now, but if you have a romantic yearning to cross the border by water, there is still one running at Drusenheim, 32km (20 miles) north of Strasbourg.
Ferries run about every 10 minutes 7am–8pm.

the Rhine valley and the river forms the border with Germany.

Saverne

Guarding the route through the hills into Alsace from Lorraine, Saverne was a town of some importance in Roman times. Nowadays, there's some of this Gallo-Roman history to be seen in the **Musée du Château du Rohan**, an imposing neoclassical palace built in 1780–90 after the previous one burnt down. Initially being the very latest in modern 18th-century refinement for the Bishop-Princes of Strasbourg, the building later served as a barracks for German troops during the annexation of Alsace and northern Lorraine after 1871, before becoming a museum in 1952. As well as the local Roman archaeological finds, there are some medieval artworks taken from other nearby castles, and a section on Louise Weiss, originally from the area, who was a writer and campaigner for

Picture-postcard Wissembourg

women's suffrage and who, at the age of 86, became a member of the first European Parliament (*Place du Général de Gaulle. Tel: 03 88 91 06 28. Open: mid-Jun–mid-Sept daily 10am–noon & 2–6pm; mid-Sept–mid-Jun Mon–Fri 2–6pm, Sat & Sun 10am–noon & 2–6pm. Admission charge*).

About 4km (2½ miles) outside Saverne, you can get a great 360-degree view of the surrounding countryside if you brave the steps up through the open-site ruins of **Château du Haut-Barr**.

Wissembourg

This pretty little town on the Lauter river owes its existence to a once-prosperous abbey (only fragments of which remain today) and its status in the 14th century as an independent town answerable only to the Holy Roman Empire. There are still some remains of the town's defensive ramparts to see, along with the impressive 13th-century **Église Saint-Pierre-et-Saint-Paul** (once part of the abbey complex) and a **Romanesque**

(*Cont. on p120*)

The Maginot Line

A defensive barrier likened to the Great Wall of China, the Maginot Line was the brainchild of André Maginot, a decorated veteran of Verdun and the Minister for War from 1929, who succeeded in persuading the French parliament to put up 3.3 billion French francs for the project. Stretching all the way along the border between Lorraine and Alsace and Germany, it was a massive engineering project built over the 1930s in preparation for just such an event as the German invasion of 1940. A system of strong points, fortifications, border guard posts, communications centres, infantry shelters, barricades, gun emplacements, supply depots and observation posts backed up a network of heavily armed *ouvrages* (fortresses or major defensive works). Maginot, who was from Lorraine, knew that there were lessons to be learnt from World War I.

One of history's biggest white elephants, however, the line proved to be pretty much useless in the end. Although the defences were connected to a Belgian fortification system, these proved to be insufficient against the might of the German army, which broke through in two days at Eben-Emael near Maastrict.

Interestingly, the line was still being manned in places after the war, forming part of Nato's Cold War defences, but by 1965 all of the forts had been abandoned. A visit to one of the massive underground fortifications is a great way to get a sense of the vastness of the scale of the project – and of the tragedy of it all being largely in vain. Most of the fortifications are buried 30m (98ft) underground and into mountainsides. The largest of them stretch out along

A World War II tank at Four à Chaux

Underground tunnels of Maginot's invention

tunnels for over 10km (6¼ miles) and house combat blocks equipped with artillery that could be fired from below ground, barracks for over 1,000 men, communications centres, officers' quarters, kitchens, sanatoriums, ammunition stores and wash blocks. Not surprisingly, given the area that some of them cover, the tunnels also have rails running along the floors, which once (and in some cases still do) carried people about the fort on electric trains.

Below is a list of some of the bigger forts along the line. If you do plan to visit, make sure that you bring warm clothing with you and note that at most of the sights you have to go as part of a guided tour (usually about two hours). English-speaking guides are usually available.

Four à Chaux at Lembach, 15km (9¼ miles) west of Wissembourg, near the German border (*Tel: 03 88 94 43 16. www.lignemaginot.fr. Guided tours only: May–Sept daily 10.30am, 2pm, 3pm & 4pm; Mar, Apr & Oct daily 2pm & 3pm; Nov–Feb Sat & Sun 2.30pm. Closed: public holidays*).

Gros ouvrage de Fermont, 15km (9¼ miles) southwest of Longwy, near the border with Belgium and Luxembourg (*Tel: 03 82 39 35 34. www.fermont.maginot.info. Guided tours only: Apr Sat & Sun 2pm & 3.30pm; May & Jun Mon–Fri 3pm, Sat & Sun 2pm & 3.30pm; Jul & Aug daily 2–4.30pm; Sept (until 3rd weekend) daily 2pm & 3.30pm; late Sept Sat & Sun 2.30pm & 3.30pm; Oct Sat & Sun 2.30pm & 4pm*).

Gros ouvrage du Hackenberg, 18.5km (11½ miles) east of Thionville, not far from the Luxembourg border (*Tel: 03 82 82 30 08. http://maginot-hackenberg.com. Guided tours only: mid-Jun–mid-Sept Mon–Fri 3pm, Sat & Sun 2pm & 3pm; Nov–Mar Sat 2pm; rest of the year Sat, Sun & public holidays 2pm*).

Ouvrage d'Artillerie de Schoenbourg, 10km (6¼ miles) south of Wissembourg (*Tel: 03 88 80 96 19. www.lignemaginot.com. Open: May–Sept daily 2–4pm; Apr & Oct Sat, Sun & public holidays 2–4pm*).

Obernai's 12th-century ramparts

About halfway down this wine route (*see pp124–5*), Colmar – like an overgrown version of one of the wine villages with its inimitably Alsatian half-timbered, flower-bedecked architecture – provides a good alternative base to Strasbourg and is a renowned centre of gastronomy. The places mentioned below are listed in geographical order from north to south.

Obernai

Obernai is a small and prosperous town 30km (19 miles) southwest of Strasbourg. It's in the heart of Alsace and in many ways is typical of the region's towns, huddled as it is around 12th-century ramparts and hemmed in beyond that by vineyards. There's not a great deal to see here in the way of official sites beyond the 13th-century Gothic **belfry** and the rather imposing neo-Gothic **Église Saint-Pierre-et-Saint-Paul** dating from 1868. However, it's a good place to stop for a slap-up Alsatian lunch (*see p187*) – the town has no fewer than two Michelin-starred restaurants – and a wander round the picturesque old streets off Place du Marché.

Barr

A little bit more down-to-earth than dinky Obernai, Barr also has some appealing architecture, especially its lovely 17th-century Hôtel de Ville (town hall) set around a courtyard. This is the setting for the town's well-known wine festival (*see p124*), which provides an

chapel, dating from the 11th century, attached to what remains of the abbey cloisters. Aside from this, the town's position on the river makes it a very pleasant stopping-off point.

Southern Vosges

South and west of Strasbourg, the Vosges mountains run north–south and reach their highest peaks in the Parc Naturel Régional des Ballons des Vosges. Lower down, on the protected, southeast-facing slopes, at an altitude of between 180m and 360m (590ft and 1,180ft), Riesling and Gewürztraminer vines thrive in the long, dry summers to produce the region's best wines, and the area is dotted with scores of ancient – and very well-kept – villages making a comfortable living out of the grapes.

excellent opportunity to taste hundreds of different wines from around the region. If you are into period interiors, there's also a fascinating museum, the **Musée de la Folie Marco** (Museum of Marco's Folly) – housed in a refined 18th-century house and laid out like a private home – which showcases local furniture and porcelain craftsmanship from the 17th to the 19th century (*30 rue du Docteur Sultzer. Tel: 03 88 08 94 72. Open: Jun–Sept Wed–Mon 10am–noon & 2–6pm; May & Oct Sat & Sun 10am–noon & 2–6pm. Admission charge*).

Sélestat

Much overlooked by its more well-known neighbour Colmar, Sélestat is a charming place with an interesting history as well as a great deal of attractive architecture dating from the 14th century onwards. The town was an important humanist centre in the 15th and 16th centuries and its corn exchange building is now a library housing two great collections of books: one from the renowned Latin school (something like an English grammar school) set up in 1452 by Ludwig Dringenberg; and the other bequeathed in 1547 by humanist scholar and friend of Erasmus, Beatus Rhenanus. The **Bibliothèque Humaniste** is visited by scholars from all over the world for its unique collection of medieval and Renaissance-era texts, but it also has displays of some of its priceless manuscripts that are open to more casual visitors, including a Merovingian lectionary dating from the 7th century, a copy of Charlemagne's capitularies

Discover the quaint town of Barr

(9th century) and an illustrated Bible dating from the 13th century (*1 rue de la Bibliothèque. Tel: 03 88 58 07 20. Open: Mon & Wed–Fri 9am–noon & 2–6pm, Sat 9am–noon (Jul & Aug also 2–5pm)*).

Riquewihr

A gem of a village in the heart of wine country, beautifully preserved Riquewihr is not without its crowds of visitors – especially at harvest time – but 16th-century winegrowers' buildings, smart houses set around courtyards, ruined ramparts and town gates, as well as its castle, make it a fun place to spend an afternoon exploring and wine tasting. The Château des Ducs de Wurtemberg dating from 1540 houses one of the town's several small

Grünewald's Isenheim Altarpiece, Colmar

THE ORIGIN OF CHRISTMAS TREES

We have the Sélestat Bibliothèque Humaniste to thank for clearing up the knotty debate about the origins of the tradition of decorating fir trees at Christmas time. The library contains a document dating from 1521 that is thought to be the first written reference to a Christmas tree, and the library puts on an exhibition each year (starting on 29 November) showing the documentary evidence first-hand and also detailing the history and evolution of the decoration of Christmas trees throughout the centuries.

museums, the **Musée de la Communication en Alsace**, which explains the history of the postal service from Roman times to the present day (*Tel: 03 89 47 93 80. Open: Apr–Oct & Dec 10am–5.30pm. Admission charge*).

Colmar

Colmar's main claim to fame is the multi-faceted Renaissance artwork known as the Isenheim Altarpiece. Painted for the nearby monastery in the village of Isenheim and now displayed as separate panels in the **Musée d'Unterlinden**, a former convent, the masterpiece draws visitors to the city from all over the world. Housed in the convent's chapel, the work was painted in 1506–15 by German artist Matthias Grünewald and vividly depicts various disturbing, traumatic and painful scenes from the life of Christ and the well-known saints Sebastian and Anthony. Truly broad in scope, the museum also holds various other Renaissance

Beautiful Riquewihr pulls in visitors all year round

treasures from the region as well as some Roman mosaics and works by Renoir and Picasso. It's a must-visit if you are in town (*1 rue d'Unterlinden. Tel: 03 89 20 15 50. www.musee-unterlinden.com. Open: May–Oct daily 9am–6pm; Nov–Apr Wed–Mon 9am–noon & 2–5pm (last entry 30 minutes before closure). Admission charge*).

Aside from the wealth of 16th-century houses to explore in the centre, the other part of town worth visiting is the area just to the south of the centre on the river Lauch known as **Petite Venise**. Formerly the tanners' district (just like in Strasbourg, *see p115*), the watery area was also used to grow fruit and vegetables in market gardens (compare with Amiens' *hortillonnages*, *see p52*). Tanning was outlawed in the 19th century and there's not much in the way of serious produce grown here now, but it's still interesting to tour the area in the old flat-bottomed boats once used to navigate the waterways (*Sweet Narcisse Boats, 10 rue de la Herse. Tel: 03 89 41 01 94. Leaves every 30 minutes, tours last about 30 minutes*).

Colmar is also famed for its cuisine and you won't have problems finding either top gastronomic flights of fancy or just very good-quality (and value) home cooking. Alternatively, if you'd rather do it yourself, why not try a cookery course while you are here (*see p127*)?

Drive: Route des vins, châteaux et abbayes

The official Route des Vins is a famous, well-signposted tour of the wine villages of southern Alsace. With the Vosges mountains serving as a stunning backdrop to the west, you can drive through picturesque, manicured vineyards and well-kept, dainty villages, stopping off for tastings as you go. That route stretches all the way from Marlenheim west of Strasbourg 130km (81 miles) south to Thann and takes about two and a half hours to drive.

The route described below takes you up into the mountains to visit monasteries and castles perched on summits as well as through some lovely vineyard landscapes. Allow a day for this trip, covering about 40km (25 miles).

Start in the little town of Obernai (see p120), 30km (19 miles) southwest of Strasbourg. From here, take the D426 signposted to Ottrott followed by the D33 signposted to Mont Sainte-Odile.

1 Mont Sainte-Odile

Perched at 764m (2,506ft) is a convent and chapel dedicated to Sainte-Odile, the patron saint of Alsace, whose father founded the nunnery here in 720. The Abbaye d'Hohenburg (Hohenburg Abbey) dates from the 17th century, and is still an important pilgrimage centre. The views over the valley from here are spectacular and the whole hilltop is surrounded by a prehistoric wall, the Mur Païen, thought by some to be over 3,000 years old.

Carry on along the D33 following signs for Barr and then turn left at the junction with the D854 to Barr.

2 Barr

Another charming and well-heeled little town (*see p120*), Barr is surrounded by

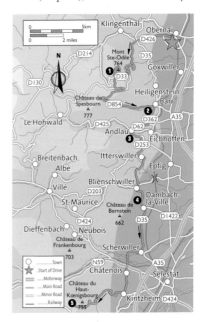

vineyards and holds a good wine festival in the second week of July.
Take the D362 out of town following signs to Mittelbergheim then turn right on to the D62 to Andlau.

3 Andlau

Andlau is a gorgeous medieval village hugged on all sides by rows of vines and is well known for its Riesling. Its wine festival happens in early July and there are even two ruined 13th-century castles to explore: Château d'Andlau and Château de Spesbourg.
Take the D253 signposted to Itterswiller and then turn left on to the D35 to Dambach-la-Ville.

4 Dambach-la-Ville

A hotchpotch of different architectural styles dating from the medieval through to the 18th century, Dambach-la-Ville is a serious wine village. Tour the cellars of the Ruhlmann estate and taste some excellent Riesling, Pinot Noir, Pinot Gris, Muscat and Gewürztraminer while you are at it (*34 rue du Maréchal Foch. Tel: 03 88 92 41 86. Open by appointment, call to book*).
Carry on along the D35 (signposted Route des Vins) through Scherwiller, Châtenois and Kintzheim, then branch off right on the D159 signposted to Haut-Kœnigsbourg.

5 Haut-Kœnigsbourg

At an altitude of over 700m (2,296ft), this is the highest bastion in the region and a superb place from which to survey Alsace – to the north, east and south. The 12th-century château was heavily restored at the beginning of the 20th century during the German occupation (*Tel: 03 88 82 50 60. www.haut-koenigsbourg.fr. Open: Jan, Feb, Nov & Dec 9.30am–noon & 1–4.30pm; Mar & Oct 9.30am–5pm; Apr, May & Sept 9.15am–5.15pm; Jun–Aug 9.15am–6pm. Admission charge*).
Retrace your route back to Obernai.

Drive: Route des vins, châteaux et abbayes

Pretty villages can be found dotted about the vineyards of southern Alsace

Eating, drinking and cooking in Alsace

It won't take you long to realise that Alsace has a distinct cuisine – one you won't find anywhere else in France

Master the local cuisine on Isabelle Sipp's cooking course

but which has quite a lot in common with food served on the eastern side of the Rhine. *Choucroute* (the French version of Sauerkraut, or pickled cabbage) is a ubiquitous listing on any *winstub* (a local term for a more informal, homely type of restaurant–bistro) menu worth its salt, and it's usually served with pork in some form, be it smoked pork shoulder, ham or sausage. Another local favourite is the *baeckoffe*, a hearty hotpot usually made with pork, mutton and beef, along with onions and potatoes or dumplings. Onions also pop up in many other Alsatian dishes and are especially delectable in a simple *tarte à l'oignon* (onion tart) or *flammekueche* (a pizza-like bread base usually topped with cream, bacon and onions) – you'll also see it listed by its French name *tarte flambée*. *Foie gras* (incredibly rich goose- or duck-liver pâté) is also highly prized in the area and you may well be offered a *foie gras bonne bouche* of some description (often as a lighter sort of mousse) before your meal. Munster, a town in the southern Vosges, is home to a strong-tasting (and smelling) unpasteurised

Treat yourself to brioche in the name of culture

producers in the region can make choosing something appropriate to go with your meal a daunting task.

The answer to this problem comes in the form of experimentation, of course, but for those with a little time to spare, a cookery course courtesy of Isabelle Sipp in Colmar comes highly recommended (*1 Grande Rue, Colmar. Tel: 06 25 99 39 40. www.cardamome. fr*). The daughter of a wine producer from nearby Niedermorschwihr, Isabelle started off in the family wine business before running wine-tasting courses and, finally, following her passion for cooking by starting up a cookery school. Her courses are open to individuals (see the website for a list of the available dates and details of the food that you will be cooking) or you can book your own privately arranged session by appointment if you can form a group of at least six people. The sessions are usually four hours long and involve cooking a three-course meal using seasonal ingredients. Afterwards, you all get to sit down and eat your creations together, accompanied by various wines – all carefully chosen by Isabelle. Although the emphasis is on the cooking (modern international cuisine, not just Alsatian food), there's no doubt that you will pick up a lot about wine from the region here too. Bon appétit!

cow's milk cheese that crops up on menus across the region.

Of course, all of this rich food, delectable as it is, is much, much better when served with some of Alsace's finest wines. Once considered to be generally low quality and fit only for local table wine, Alsatian viticulture has had a renaissance in the last 40 years or so and there are now several world-class wines to look out for. But seven main grape varieties, three Appellations d'Origine Contrôlée (AOCs) and hundreds of

Getting away from it all

France is far less densely populated than most other countries in western Europe, so it's pretty easy to escape the crowds. And although parts of the northeast have more people per square kilometre than most other areas of the country, there's still plenty of open, empty countryside to explore. And, like the rest of France, there's a huge variety of different landscapes, from windswept coastlines to rolling forests and high mountains.

Picardy
Forêt de Compiègne and Forêt de Laigue

A massive oak and beech forest to the east of Compiègne, the **Forêt de Compiègne** is the third biggest in France and was once the hunting ground of the kings who stayed in the château there. Covering an area of

Wading birds at the Parc du Marquenterre

14,417 hectares (35,625 acres) and encompassing several pretty villages, like Vieux Moulin and Pierrefonds (*see p55*), the forest contains over 1,200km (745 miles) of paths, some of them laid out by François I over 500 years ago. They were once used for hunting wild boar (sadly now hunted to extinction here) and deer, but these days you are more likely to meet cyclists whizzing along the paths. It can get busy on the main drags at weekends and in the summer holidays, but it's easy enough to find yourself alone in the woods if you want to get off the more beaten tracks – just make sure that you have a map with you if you decide to go wandering. The Beaux Monts hills southeast of the château have an uninterrupted view of the palace about 4km (2½ miles) away.

The **Forêt de Laigue**, which lies to the northeast on the other side of the Ainse river, is smaller but wilder and less busy. It's especially lovely in spring and early summer, when the ground is carpeted

Stray from the beaten track in the verdant Forêt de Compiègne

with bluebells and other wild flowers. Autumn is hunting season – beware.

Parc du Marquenterre, Picardy

Lying between the two huge estuaries of the Somme and the Authie rivers, the Parc du Marquenterre is an eerie salt marsh sandwiched between sand dunes and pine forests that has been gradually reclaimed from the sea over the last eight centuries. Used for grazing sheep and cattle (highly prized for their sea-salty flavour), the area is also an important habitat for migratory wading birds. A protected nature reserve, it covers only 260 hectares (642 acres) but plays host

(at various different times of the year) to an astonishing 360 species of birds. To put that in perspective, there are only around 600 species found in the whole of Europe. You can explore the area on your own or as part of a tour guided by an expert ornithologist. It's also possible to ride the locally bred Henson horses across the beach sands.

25 bis chemin des Garennes, Saint-Quentin-en-Tourmont. Tel: 03 22 25 68 99. Open: mid-Jan–Mar & mid-Nov–Dec 10am–6pm (ticket office closes at 3pm); Apr–Sept 10am–7.30pm (ticket office closes at 5pm); Oct–mid-Nov 10am–6pm (ticket office closes at 4pm).

More information (and walking maps) are available from the tourist office in Compiègne (*Place de l'Hôtel de Ville. Tel: 03 44 40 01 00. www.compiegne-tourisme.fr*).

Champagne-Ardenne
Lakes of the Champagne Humide

East of Troyes lies a clay basin quite different from the chalky plateau around Reims and Épernay to the north. The low-lying and humid area has several man-made reservoirs built in the 1960s and 1970s (feeding Paris as well as the local area) that now form important habitats for migrating birds and other fauna as well as providing thousands of hectares of protected-status nature park to explore.

To the south lies the chain of reservoirs and ancient watery woodland known as the Parc Naturel Régional de la Forêt d'Orient. The three lakes (d'Orient, du Temple and Amance) were created when the Seine and Aube rivers were diverted, and together they now cover a vast 5,000 hectares (12,355 acres). Lac d'Orient has a small marina on it if you feel like sailing, and you can also go diving and windsurfing here. The middle reservoir, Lac du Temple, is quieter and forms the main part of the bird sanctuary. Over 250 different bird species are thought to visit the region at various times of the year, including thousands of cranes in autumn, stopping over on their way south from Scandinavia to winter in Africa. Lac Amance to the northeast is for petrol

heads: here you can waterski and jet ski without disturbing the peace of the other two lakes, where power boats are prohibited. Away from the lakes, the Forêt d'Orient is an extraordinary (mainly oak and hornbeam) woodland habitat partially inundated with water. Throughout the forest you will find ponds where carp, pike and roach have been bred for hundreds of years by locals and are still fished. The forest also provides a unique ecosystem for a wealth of fauna, including salamanders, palmate newts and yellow-bellied toads. It's also possible to camp in the park. For more information on hiking trails and other activities, contact the Maison du Parc in Piney, about 7km (4¼ miles) north of Lac d'Orient (*Tel: 03 25 43 81 90. www.pnr-foret-orient.fr*).

Lac du Der-Chantecoq, about 55km (34 miles) northeast of Lac d'Orient, is another reservoir, this time created from the Marne river. At 4,800 hectares (11,860 acres), it's the biggest single man-made lake in western Europe and also provides a much-needed stopping-over point for migrating birds – especially cranes, some of which stay here throughout the winter. You can do pretty much any kind of watersport on the lake (including sailing, windsurfing and waterskiing), and there are hiking and cycle paths around its edges and into the ancient Forêt de Der ('der' means oak in old Gaullish, although there are also many hornbeams, wild cherries and ash trees here too). Contact the Lac du Der tourist office for more information, maps and activity details (*Giffaumont Champaubert. Tel: 03 26 72 62 80. www.lacduder.com*).

Vallée de la Meuse

The dark, wooded hills of the Ardennes are very sparsely populated and, with the exception of the Vosges, have some of the most unspoilt landscape in the whole region. Especially beautiful is the meandering valley of the Meuse river north of Charleville-Mézières, which cuts its way dramatically through the steep hills on its journey to join up with the Rhine and ultimately head out into the north sea (in The Netherlands). There's loads to do in the area, from exhilarating mountain biking, rock climbing and hiking to gentler pursuits such as fishing and trips down the river. There's also a cycle way that runs for 83km (51 miles) from Givet south along an old tow path to Charleville-Mézières.

Around the village of Monthermé, where the Meuse meets the Semoy river, you can climb up several rocky outcrops poking up through the treetops that make for superb viewpoints over a forest that seems to stretch on forever. The Roche aux Sept Villages, situated 3km (1¾ miles) south of Monthermé on the D989, provides incredible views of the snaking Meuse

Escape to the rippling waters of Lac du Der-Chantecoq

Le Parc Naturel Régional des Ballons des Vosges

river and, as its name suggests, of the seven villages dotted along its course. Beyond this outcrop, you can hike to Longue Roche (about 30 minutes away) for even more spectacular views. The Roc de la Tour – drive 6km (3¾ miles) east of Monthermé on the D31, then turn left on the Route Forestière de la Lyre – is another strange outcrop that almost looks like the ruins of some ancient fort (and abounds in legends about a local lord who sold his soul to the devil). From here, you can take various different hikes through the wooded valleys.

For further details, visit the tourist office in Charleville-Mézières or Monthermé, both of which can provide a vast amount of information about the area and also help with booking various activities and tours:

Office de Tourisme Charleville-Mézières, 24 place Ducale, Charleville-Mézières. Tel: 03 24 56 06 08. www.ardennes.com. Office de Tourisme des Vallées de Meuse et Semoy, place J B Clément, Monthermé. Tel: 03 24 54 46 73.

Lorraine and Alsace
Delta de la Sauer
Tucked away between Munchhausen and Seltz (two villages on the Rhine in the north of Alsace) is a strange, otherworldly and almost jungle-like wetland formed from a change in course of the Sauer river following drainage work carried out on the Rhine in the 19th century. It has created a unique habitat and possibly one of the last remaining sanctuaries for many native Rhineland animal and plant species. The species count includes 183 species of bird, lots of amphibians (especially green tree frogs, which you can hear loudly chirruping away in mating season), rare wild flowers, and a diverse woodland of oak, ash, willow and poplar. Starting at Munchhausen (where there's an information centre), there's a cycleway through the reserve which will take you all the way to Seltz about 5km (3 miles) away, or you can loop around the waterways and double back on yourself to get to the banks of the Rhine.

La Réserve Naturelle Delta de la Sauer, 42 route du Rhin, Munchhausen. Tel: 03 88 59 77 00. www.nature-munchhausen.com

Le Parc Naturel Régional des Ballons des Vosges

The Vosges mountains change shape and size the further south in the range you go. The sandstone gives way to granite and the peaks here have been rounded by weather over millions of years into 'ballons' rather than sharp points. Nevertheless, they are twice – and in some cases three times – as high as the hills of the northern Vosges. South and west of Obernai, there's a more Alpine feel to the hills, with their winding switchback roads, deep coniferous woods and gentle mountain pastures that are an almost dazzlingly intense green colour. Come in late spring and summer and there's a profusion of wild flowers here; in autumn, the hills can often be shrouded in mist; and by the end of November, many of the passes are closed to cars as the snow falls by the metre. This, of course, brings skiers (both cross-country and downhill) to the region's small ski resorts (*see p160*), and the Route des Crêtes stretching 80km (50 miles) from north to south (*see pp106–7*) becomes a superb cross-country trail. In summer, the mountains are popular with walkers and there are hiking trails to suit various different levels of fitness. As well as the big peaks of the area –

A marvellous vista over Lac d'Alfeld from Le Ballon d'Alsace

Getting away from it all

The ruins of Château de Falkenstein

Le Col du Grand Ballon at 1,424m (4,672ft), Le Hohneck at 1,364m (4,475ft), Le Petit Ballon at 1,267m (4,156ft), Le Ballon d'Alsace at 1,247m (4,091ft) and Le Ballon de Servance at 1,216m (3,989ft) – there are valleys, mountain lakes and streams, and sweeping glacial cirques to explore. In Munster, 20km (12½ miles) west of Colmar, and the town that gives its name to the cow's cheese made in the nearby mountain pastures, you'll find the Maison du Parc and all the information you need to make the most of your visit (*1 cour de l'Abbaye, Munster. Tel: 03 89 77 90 34. www.parc-ballons-vosges.fr*).

Le Parc Naturel Régional des Vosges du Nord

The northern Vosges has been protected by its status as a regional park since 1975. The park covers an area of steep hills, forests and, in the northwest around Bitche and Volmunster, part of the high, rolling Lorraine plateau. The area is especially good for hiking, biking and horse riding, and there are various nature and heritage trails that you can follow to discover the region's varied wildlife, including wild boar, roe deer and even lynx. There are also many hilltop castles, quiet, welcoming little villages and, at Vieux Windstein, even troglodyte houses.

The forest is a mixture of deciduous oak and beech and evergreen pines and spruces, interspersed with rocky outcrops on which you'll find ruined castles like Château de Falkenstein and Château de Fleckenstein to remind you that this is border country. You can swim in the lake at Étang de Hanau, a clearing in the Forêt de Hanau, and then follow trails around the lake to the extraordinary Erbsenfelsen natural stone arch sticking up out of the trees. And just off the D3 outside Climbach,

on the way to Wissembourg, is a hiking path up to the Col du Pigeonnier, which at 432m (1,417ft), has spectacular views of the Alsace plain below. In the south of the park, the village of La Petite Pierre has a Maison du Parc where you can pick up detailed information and maps before setting out to explore on foot or by car (*Tel: 03 88 01 49 59. www.parc-vosges-nord.fr*), and the other villages in the park also have tourist offices which can provide useful information.

Marvel at the natural beauty of the northern Vosges

Getting away from it all

When to go

People don't go to northern France for the weather. Just as in England, the climate here is considered by most nationals to be cold and damp in winter, and merely damp in summer. But this isn't the whole story and, again, as in England, the weather here can turn on the charm – there can be glorious springs and summers, as well as crisp, cold winters.

August is a very busy month – with both foreign and domestic visitors – and is best avoided if possible. Ironically, it's also the time when a lot of tourist-related businesses, such as hotels and restaurants, are closed.

Climate

There are regional variations and microclimates, of course, but, generally speaking, if you intend to spend a lot of time outdoors, spring or early summer is a good time to visit. At this time, the temperature is usually warm enough to do away with coats (although not sweaters) and the countryside is at its most breathtaking. Late summer and early autumn (August to mid-September) can bring humid weather and some spectacular thunderstorms the further south you go. In autumn, the temperature drops rapidly but the forested areas (for example, around Compiègne, in the Ardennes and the northern Vosges) are stunning in late

September and October. Winter is colder still, but not necessarily any wetter than it is in the summer. There's usually a couple of metres of snowfall in the high Vosges from around mid-December until mid-March.

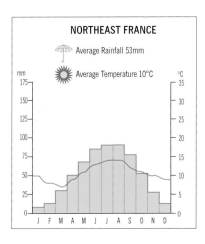

NORTHEAST FRANCE

Average Rainfall 53mm

Average Temperature 10°C

WEATHER CONVERSION CHART

25.4mm = 1 inch

°F = 1.8 × °C + 32

Seasonal sports

All watersports on the lakes and on the Côte d'Opale are generally summertime activities – and often require wetsuits even then. For walkers, the mountains of the Vosges and Ardennes have different appeals at different times of year: go in later May and June for burgeoning green countryside and a carpet of wild flowers, and in late September and October for autumnal flair. The ski season in the Vosges usually starts just before Christmas and lasts until March – depending on the amount of snowfall. For up-to-date snow reports in winter, visit *www.onthesnow.co.uk*

Holidays and special events

Expect the main holiday times in France (Easter, August, the late October–early November holiday around La Toussaint (All Saints' Day), Christmas and New Year) to be busy. That means that roads and major tourist sites will be more crowded, and hotels and restaurants more likely to be booked up well in advance. December is a great time to visit if you are in a festive mood and fancy a shopping trip, as all of the region's main cities put on big Christmas fairs – but again, this does draw in the crowds. Strasbourg's fair is especially well known and the city can be very lively or a little too overcrowded, depending on your point of view. The wine harvest (from mid-September to mid-October) is a wonderful time to visit Alsace and Champagne if you want to get a feel for the wine-producing business in action. Everywhere you go in the area you'll see people out in the vineyards picking the grapes, and there are also many wine fairs around this time, but it can mean that the smaller producers are very busy and therefore not able to spend as much time showing you around their cellars.

For more information on wine festivals and other events worth timing your visit for, see 'Festivals and events' pp20–21, or check the regional tourist boards' websites (see p153).

Cross your fingers for some sun at Malo-les-Bains

Getting around

France has an excellent road network and makes a great 'driving holiday' destination. Having said that, though, traffic in and around the main cities (especially Lille and Strasbourg) can be gridlocked at peak times and, given that there is also a very good rail service to most small towns throughout the region, it's worth considering taking the train if you are not planning to visit out-of-the-way villages and remote countryside.

By car

Bringing a car to northern France from the UK is easy, so it makes some sense to drive here rather than fly. The roads are, generally speaking, in excellent condition and the motorways (*autoroutes*) provide a useful network of fast, and often empty, highways between most of the major cities in the region. Note, however, that the majority of them are toll roads and you will be required to stop at toll booths (*péages*) periodically or when you come off the motorway.

The alternative is to come by Eurostar and pick up a hire car in Lille (about an hour and a half from London St Pancras). Most car hire companies are represented at Lille Europe train station (where the Eurostar service stops): expect to spend about €30–40 per day for a basic model. Parking on the street in towns is usually metered and there are now many city-centre underground carparks as well.

Legal requirements

Driving is on the right and it is a legal requirement that everyone in the car wears a seat belt (children must have age-appropriate car seats). You must carry on you the vehicle registration documents as well as your car insurance details, driving licence (a UK one is valid for France) and, ideally, your passport. The speed limits for French roads are as follows: 130km/h for *autoroutes* (or 110km/h if it is raining); 110km/h on dual carriageways; 90km/h on other roads outside built-up areas; and 50km/h in built-up areas unless otherwise stated (in some town centres this is reduced to 30km/h). Note that there has been a vigorous speed enforcement campaign in recent years and you will see almost as many speed cameras in France as you do in the UK. Other legal requirements for your car (that will be checked if you are stopped by the police) are that you have a GB sticker on the outside of the car, a warning triangle, spare headlight bulbs, a first-aid kit and a fluorescent safety vest. All of this kit can be bought at the ferry and Eurotunnel terminals in Britain. If you are driving your own right-hand-drive car, it is also a good idea to attach anti-dazzle stickers (available at most service stations in Britain and at ferry and Eurotunnel terminals) to your headlights – otherwise you will dazzle oncoming traffic even if your headlights are dipped.

Public transport
Air
There are a few direct **Air France** (*www.airfrance.co.uk*) flights between Lille and Strasbourg (one hour) but otherwise flying is not really an option for getting around this region.

Follow the signs to avoid losing your way on winding town-centre streets

Bicycle

Cycling is a hugely popular sport in France but, strangely, it has taken a while to catch on as a means of everyday transport in towns. There are not usually that many cycle lanes in cities – the big exception to this rule being Strasbourg – but most towns do now have a Paris *vélib*-style public street cycle hire system. You will need a credit card to hire a bike (a deposit will be held on your card until you have returned the bike) but the hire cost is usually only a couple of euros for an hour or so.

Bus and tram

Intercity bus services in this region of France are generally limited to places that are not on the rail network and they are run by a number of different private companies. Look for signs to the *gare routière* (bus station) if you need to travel by bus but, generally speaking, people use the train or cars for getting between towns if possible. In towns, however, you will usually find decent bus services and, in bigger cities like Lille, Reims and Strasbourg, also tram or metro services. Most towns have a local ticketing system and it is worth checking with the tourist office about day passes and other fares because it will almost certainly be cheaper than buying a single ticket on board (for which you need to have the correct change). However, you will find that all of the towns covered in this book (including Lille and Strasbourg)

have centres that are easily managed on foot if you are reasonably fit.

Taxi

Most towns have a metered taxi service with a taxi rank outside the train station. Taxis are usually pretty cheap and are worth considering as an alternative to buses and trams – especially if you have luggage. If you are looking for a taxi service, your hotel or the local tourist office will be able to help.

Train

Widely used, the French rail network is excellent and has been significantly improved in recent years by the high-speed TGV (Train à Grande Vitesse) services that operate between the bigger cities and Paris and also between some of these regional capitals. Strasbourg is under two hours from Champagne-Ardenne TGV station (just outside Reims) and it's possible to get from Lille Europe to Champagne-Ardenne TGV in about the same amount of time. Note that you have to book all TGV journeys in advance (either online or at a station). **Rail Europe** has a useful English-language website if you want to book online (*www.raileurope.co.uk*), and the ticket machines at TGV stations are easy to use and have English-language options too. As in Britain, the earlier you book your tickets, the cheaper they will usually be, and off-peak journeys can be considerably cheaper than they are at peak times. The standard TER rail

Take advantage of France's excellent and extensive network of trains

network is much cheaper than the TGV, but it is also very reliable and serves a much wider network of towns throughout the region. It's not necessary to book these tickets in advance but, again, may be cheaper if you do. If you are planning to do a lot of train travel, it may be worth considering a rail pass (*see the Rail Europe website for details*).

All train stations in France have automatic ticket machines where you can book and buy tickets, and they all have English-language options on them. One important thing to remember when you are travelling by train is that you must validate (*composter*) your ticket before you board the train. There are yellow machines, which stamp and validate your ticket, by the entrances to most platforms. If you do forget to stamp your ticket before boarding, make sure that you speak to the conductor of the train as soon as you can – otherwise you may incur a fine.

Accommodation

As the world's top tourist destination, France is well equipped when it comes to accommodating its visitors. Like the rest of the country, the northeast region has a broad range of places to stay, from lavish 5-star hotels in its cities to basic (and not-so-basic) campsites and mountain refuges deep in the heart of its forests and on secluded mountain trails.

Refreshingly, in comparison with Britain (and some other European countries), prices are generally reasonable and good value at both ends of the accommodation budget. At peak holiday times (especially in August), you are strongly advised to book your accommodation well in advance. If you need help finding a hotel in a town, the local tourist office will be able to advise and also book a hotel room for you.

Hotels

Hotels come in all shapes and sizes, of course, and you will find that a government-regulated star-ranking system is used (1-star being the most basic sort of room that might not necessarily have a private bathroom, 5-star being top-of-the-range luxury hotels with facilities like 24-hour room service, restaurants and porters). This star system is no indication of charm, however, so it's worth doing some research beforehand if you can. Almost all towns will have at least one chain hotel in them: brands like **Best Western** are at the higher end of the scale; **Mercure** and **Holiday Inn** chains are mid-range, **Ibis** usually cheaper still; and **Formule1** are the cheapest, offering clean, secure rooms for as little as €25 per night.

If you would rather stay away from chains, then you should not have too much trouble finding a small, sometimes family-run, hotel in most town centres across the region. The **Logis de France** (*www.logishotels.com*) is a label worth looking out for – these are smaller, usually 1- and 2-star independent hotels. 'Boutique' hotels, often with an emphasis on contemporary design, are also springing up in many larger cities such as Lille, Strasbourg, Reims, Metz and Nancy. They usually have fewer than 20 rooms and are often located in interesting historic buildings. Outside town and city centres, you can sometimes find upmarket

Experience French hospitality in one of the region's small hotels

accommodation in large country houses and historic châteaux – often also with large gardens to explore. **Relais & Chateau** (*www.relais chateaux.com*) and **Relais du Silence** (*www.relaisdusilence.com*) are both useful websites worth consulting if this is the kind of accommodation you are after.

Chambres d'hôtes

Offering a maximum of five rooms and usually in someone's private house, these are roughly the equivalent of a Bed and Breakfast establishment in Britain, and their quality and price can be just as varied as they are in the UK. Some of them, in 18th-century châteaux, for example, are very luxurious and offer huge, beautifully decorated rooms with four-poster beds, all the mod cons you'd expect from a 5-star hotel (such as TV, mini-bar and Wi-Fi, although without room service), and big en-suite bathrooms stuffed with fluffy towels. Others are much more humble but will at least offer you a room with a private bathroom. Breakfast (which these days usually includes fresh fruit, yoghurt, bread and pastries, as well as cold meat and cheese) is included in the price. Generally speaking, this sort of accommodation represents very good value for money (even the most expensive ones are unlikely to be more than €120). Another big bonus is the fact that you will get a much more personal welcome than you would in a hotel, and you can thus often experience a real sense of warm French hospitality and friendship. A good online resource for this kind of accommodation is the website *www.chambresdhotesdecharme.com*

Self-catering

Rural *gîte* self-catering is a very popular type of accommodation with French tourists, and increasingly with foreign visitors too. You can get a lot more for your money than you can in hotels and *chambres d'hôtes* and, in general, self-catering holiday rentals in this part of France are cheap compared with other western European countries. Prices, of course, vary hugely and you can find houses with big gardens and swimming

Pitch your tent at one of northeast France's ubiquitous campsites

pools that will sleep more than ten people as well as tiny one-bedroom cottages. Bear in mind that in high season (usually Easter, August, All Saints' Day and Christmas–New Year), prices are often as much as double what they are in low season. Some of this self-catering accommodation must be rented for a minimum of a week (usually from Saturday to Saturday) but it is often possible to rent just for a weekend or for a few days mid-week in low season. The **Gîtes de France** website (*www.gites-de-france.com*) has a huge list of self-catering holiday cottages to choose from. **Chez Nous** (*www.cheznous.com*) is another useful website for self-catering properties (many of which are second homes owned by English people).

Camping

Almost all villages in France have a campsite, and camping is popular with domestic and international visitors. In the height of summer, especially, be aware of this and make sure that you book a pitch well in advance. **Camping France** (*www.campingfrance.com*) is a great website with a comprehensive list of campsites the length and breadth of France. Some campsites are very well equipped with electricity, hot and cold water, luxurious wash blocks and swimming pools, while others are much more basic. This variation is usually reflected in the price, which starts from around €10 per night for a pitch, but it's worth checking online first if you are concerned about the level of facilities. Campsites often have chalet-type accommodation too, for those who might want a night off from being under canvas. Note that many campsites are closed from the end of October until March.

If you prefer the convenience of a campervan to the joys of pitching and dismantling tents, rental is possible in big cities like Lille and Strasbourg. Check websites such as *www.family campervanrentals-france.com* for details of locations and prices. If you wish to camp 'wild', away from campsites, make sure that you get the permission of the landowner before even thinking about pitching your tent or parking your campervan. It is illegal to camp on private land without permission.

Mountain refuges

If you are serious about walking in the Vosges, then it's worth considering staying in refuges. These are usually pretty basic, providing bunk-type shared accommodation, sometimes a hot meal, and often with a cosy little bar too. Prices start from as little as €15 for bed and breakfast. As with camping, it is important to book in advance in high season, and in any case you should phone ahead if at all possible to check that the refuge is open and, if necessary, that it is serving a hot meal. **Gîtes Refuges** (*www.gites-refuges.com*) has a comprehensive list of refuges throughout France.

Food and drink

In a country renowned the world over for its cuisine, the northeast region of France can certainly hold its head up high when it comes to the quality – and variety – of its dishes. Generally speaking, the food is heartier than you'll find in the south, but don't confuse that with a lack of subtlety or sophistication. And if it's fine wine you're after, you'll not go far wrong in Champagne or Alsace.

Regional specialities

As in the rest of France, in the northeast you will find a great deal of diversity. In Flanders in the Nord-Pas-de-Calais region, many homes and restaurants serve a great deal of the sort of coastal and Low Country fare you'd expect to see in Belgium. There are several excellent *moules-frites* (mussels and chips) – and other seafood – restaurants in and around Lille and along the coast, and seafood such as eel (*anguille*) and smoked herrings (*craquelots*) abound. Other Flemish dishes include stews such as *hochepot* (a hotpot of usually veal, mutton or pork and vegetables), *carbonade* (usually beef braised in beer) and *potjevleesch* (known usually as just *potch* in French Flanders, this is a combination of rabbit or chicken and veal and pork potted and preserved in jelly – a bit like a pork pie without the pastry) served cold with chips and beer. Picardy is well known for its soups – made with just about everything (including frogs' legs and tripe) depending upon the season. Maroilles is a local cheese from the region which is often on the menu in Picardy. It comes in many different forms but often in a creamy sauce to accompany pork or veal dishes. As you might expect, Alsace has a distinctly German flavour with *choucroute* (sauerkraut or pickled cabbage) featuring heavily on *winstub* (restaurant-bistro) menus throughout the region. It is usually served with various types of pork (sausages, chops, bacon or ham). *Foie gras* (goose- or duck-liver pâté) is another local favourite in Alsace and Lorraine – as is one of France's most famous dishes: *quiche Lorraine*, which is made with cream, eggs and bacon. In Champagne, you can expect to find the eponymous sparkling wine used as an ingredient in many dishes – both sweet and savoury – and *andouillette* (chitterling sausage) is another ubiquitous menu item. Finally, the woody Ardennes is famous for its game, from wild boar and venison to pigeon, woodcock and even songbirds like thrush.

Where to eat

From top-flight Michelin-starred restaurants to the simplest *auberge* (inn) or bistro, you will generally find that you have plenty of options when it comes to choosing somewhere to eat.

Cafés in towns usually have little more than a snack menu including sandwiches and perhaps a few cooked dishes or *plats du jour*, but they are good places to come for breakfast, when they will serve fresh croissants and other pastries with your coffee. Brasseries, like cafés, are often large places that you'll find in towns and they usually serve lots of classic and simple

Fill your glass (and your car boot) with the region's famous produce

Treat yourself to the offerings of a pâtisserie

French dishes (including *steak-frites* or grilled fish, for example). Bistros are usually smaller, cosier restaurants and often will be popular hang-outs for locals in areas that are off the beaten track. Restaurants and *auberges* are often slightly more formal places (although, of course, they range from simple rural inns to chic and glitzy city establishments) where you may find more regional specialities and less regular opening hours (*see below*).

When to eat

As a rule, opening hours for bistros and restaurants are noon–2pm and 7.30–9.30pm: if listings in this guide state that a venue is open for 'lunch & dinner' (*see 'Directory'*), you should assume these hours. Most French people eat quite early – often sitting down to lunch at noon and dinner at 7.30pm. Many places are shut at least one day a week (often Sunday or Monday) and may not be open in the evening during the week. Cafés and brasseries are often open all day long (from 8 or 9am until 10 or 11pm) but may have restricted menus (if they are serving food at all) at certain times of day.

Wine and beer

Naturally, in Alsace you may well find a bias towards the local wines, served both before and with your meal, and no bar or restaurant in Champagne would think of offering you anything other than champagne as an apéritif. It's worth experimenting with different local labels and grape varieties while you are eating – especially if you are planning to buy wine to take home with you (for more on this, *see* '*Shopping*', *pp154–5* & '*Champagne houses in Reims*', *pp66–7*). Beer is also popular in the region, particularly in French Flanders and Alsace (where most of the beer that is produced in France is made). Brands to look out for include Fischer and Karlsbräu. Most beers are served draught (*à la pression*), but in Strasbourg you will find several specialist beer bars serving hundreds of bottled beers (from both France and Belgium).

Markets

Despite the out-of-town shopping complexes and supermarkets, food markets are still an important part of life in France, and almost all towns will hold a market of some sort at least once a week. Produce varies from region to region and from season to season, but at a typical local market you can expect to find delicious fresh vegetables and fruit (and fresh bottled juice) plus charcuterie, cheese, bread, fresh meat and sometimes fish, as well as all manner of local specialities.

Vegetarians

Vegetarians will have a tough time eating out in France. You will usually find that there is only one vegetarian option on the menu (if you are lucky), which means that you often end up having to eat something that you do not necessarily want. Having said that, the concept of vegetarianism (in foreigners) is significantly more widely appreciated now than it was a decade ago, which means that if you explain that you cannot eat meat ('*Je suis végétarien(ne). Avez-vous quelque chose sans viande?*' – 'I am vegetarian. Do you have anything without meat?'), the chef will always offer you something else if there is nothing on the menu that you can eat. If you are self-catering, however, you can stock up on a huge variety of tasty and locally grown fresh fruit and vegetables at your local market (*see above*).

Tipping

Almost no restaurants include service on the bill, so a 10 per cent tip will be appreciated. Of course, you can always leave more if you think the service especially deserved it. If service is included, you do not need to leave anything extra.

Entertainment

Depending upon where in the region you are, you'll find that entertainment, and nightlife in particular, takes many different forms. The bigger cities covered in this book all have a healthy collection of bars, live music venues, theatres, cinemas and a packed calendar of festivals and events. Outside the cities, however, evening entertainment is normally a more muted affair based around the local village bar.

That said, it's entirely possible that you'll stumble upon a raucous village festival, especially if you are visiting in the summer.

Bars and clubs

The French are not known for being big-drinking night owls in general and it is only in large towns with a sizeable student population (such as Lille, Strasbourg and Nancy) that you will find a decent selection of late-night bars. British and Irish-style pubs and wine bars are popular in all of the bigger cities listed in this guide and they can get busy later on in the evening, when live music is often a feature (usually one night a week unless the venue is specifically a music bar), but most places will close at around 1am, perhaps later at the weekend. Nightclubs are also a feature of city life, of course, but compared with London or Paris it's a small scene, even in places like Lille and Strasbourg.

Cinema

All small and medium-sized towns will have at least one cinema, but you may find that (like Britain) they are large multiplexes and often outside of the town centres. In larger cities, you will have much more choice in the centre of town and you will almost always find at least one cinema that shows films in the original language with French subtitles (rather than those that are dubbed into French). These are often smaller, independent places with more art-house leanings, an international programme and often an annual film festival. Strasbourg, with its cosmopolitan, multilingual population, is a good place to find cinemas showing films in their original language. (*See 'Directory' listings for details of cinemas showing original-language films.*)

Local festivals

Festivals throughout the region come in all different shapes, themes and sizes, from big international gatherings to tiny village celebrations little bigger than a street party. One thing you can be sure of is that you are unlikely to be too far away from a festival of some sort or another – especially in summer. Throughout wine country in Alsace and Champagne, for example, every little village will have a *fête des vins* at least once a year (and very often twice) where you will get a chance not only to taste scores of different wines but also, usually, many other local delicacies. As well as these produce-based local agricultural festivals, very often there are also parties thrown in villages and towns across the region on certain important national holidays, especially 14 July (Bastille Day) and 15 August (Feast of the Assumption). If you are lucky enough to be in the right place at the right time, these can be a great way to get to know the locals, their food and their customs. It's also a great value-for-money night out, with food, drink and entertainment all costing less than a meal for one would in even a modest restaurant.

Performing arts

There's a great deal to see in terms of performing arts (be it theatre, opera, classical music, ballet or contemporary dance, or gigs at less formal music venues) in this part of France and it is

Live music in Metz

Enjoy a multifarious entertainment scene across the region's cities

well worth doing some research into what is on before you go (tickets sell out fast – especially for more popular classical music performances). Lille, Reims, Nancy, Metz and Strasbourg are all richly endowed when it comes to venues and all have varied and often cutting-edge programmes. Lille is home to one of France's national orchestras and the internationally acclaimed Ballet du Nord a few kilometres outside at Roubaix. Reims has a beautifully restored theatre and an important music festival, Les Flâneries Musicales de Reims. Metz has France's oldest working theatre, as well as L'Arsenal, a contemporary music and dance venue, and a growing programme of live performances at the new Centre Pompidou-Metz. And Nancy is home to another renowned orchestra, l'Orchestre National de Lorraine, based in the opera building on Place Stanislas. Strasbourg really shines when it comes to live music, with a great selection of venues (such as the Palais de la Musique, the Musée d'Art Moderne et Contemporain, and the Opéra National du Rhin and its jazz venue La Laiterie) as well as a string of festivals throughout the year. For more details about specific events and venues, visit the regional and local tourist board websites (see below) or check out the online listings at *www.spectacles-publications.com*

In terms of hearing live rock and pop music in bars and clubs, Nancy and Strasbourg, with their big student populations, are probably the best places to go.

Outside the big cities, choice is obviously more limited, but it is often possible to hear live choral and organ recitals in churches (check their notice boards for details of upcoming performances, often in the evenings or on Sunday mornings) and at the many local village festivals throughout the region.

Son et lumière

A fashion that has gone from strength to strength over the last decade, high-tech *son et lumière* (literally 'sound and light') shows are popping up in city centres all over the region. They are usually only summer (and sometimes Christmas) events and take place at different times of the evening depending upon when it gets dark –

check with the various tourist offices for further details. In Amiens, the façade of the cathedral is spectacularly brought back to its polychromatic former medieval glory with a show that is based on painstaking research carried out when the recent restoration work was done (see *www.amiens-cathedrale.com*). Nancy's beautiful Place Stanislas is the backdrop for another show, *Rendez-vous Place Stanislas*, this time based more on popular historical themes but no less charismatic (see *www.rendez-vous.nancy.fr*). Metz does not have a sound-and-light show, but its award-winning lighting design seems to 'paint' most of the yellow stone medieval buildings in the centre and along the river in swathes of honey-coloured light.

Regional tourist boards

The regional tourist boards and main city tourist offices are great sources of information on local festivals and events:

Alsace (*www.tourisme-alsace.com*)
Champagne-Ardenne (*www.tourisme-champagne-ardenne.com*)
Lille (*www.lilletourism.com*)
Lorraine (*www.tourisme-lorraine.fr*)
Metz (*http://tourisme.mairie-metz.fr*)
Nancy (*www.ot-nancy.fr*)
Nord–Pas-de-Calais (*www.northernfrance-tourism.com*)
Picardy (*http://picardietourisme.com*)
Reims (*www.reims-tourism.com*)
Strasbourg (*www.otstrasbourg.fr*)
Troyes (*www.tourism-troyes.com*)

Shopping

Whether you are looking for an antique bargain in a flea market, fresh ingredients for your picnic at a local town market or a good deal on a case or two of wine direct from a producer, the chances are that you'll find shopping in France a pleasure. Not surprisingly, food and drink are most people's priorities and you won't have to look very far to find all manner of local delicacies for sale.

For something a little longer lasting, an *objet d'art* made of glass is a particularly good choice of souvenir. Glassware – whether for buildings or objects in the home – is an important industry in this part of France, hardly surprisingly given the number of Gothic churches and cathedrals.

Arts and crafts

Boutique Daum is the official outlet for the Daum glass factory and stocks the very latest designs (*14 place Stanislas, Nancy. Tel: 03 83 32 21 65. www.daum.fr*).

Centre d'International d'Art Verrier sells glass baubles in Christmas markets throughout the region (*see below*) and at tourist offices in Lorraine and Alsace (*Place Robert Schuman, Meisenthal (halfway between Metz and Strasbourg in the northern Vosges). Tel: 03 87 96 87 16*).

Imagerie d'Épinal is a fascinating print museum (based in the old print works that made the town famous)

with a vast collection of prints for sale (*42 bis Quai de Dogneville, Épinal. Tel: 03 29 34 21 87*).

Clothes

Nancy, Lille and Strasbourg are probably the best places to shop if you are after new designs. You will find all of the usual French (and international) high-street chains as well as a few interesting independent shops.

Troyes is well known for its large number of factory fashion outlet shops. **Marques Avenue** has scores of brands for sale at between 30 and 70 per cent of their retail price (*114 boulevard de Dijon, Saint-Julien-les-Villas (a couple of kilometres south of Troyes centre). Tel: 03 25 82 80 80*).

Food and drink

The larger cities all have at least one food market (*see below*). This is often a covered permanent building (usually known as 'Les Halles') that may be open for business five or six days a week and has stallholders selling everything from all the basics to local specialities. Markets are a great place to get a sense of the regional differences – and also of price. It's worth shopping around: you may find that the local delicatessen's prices compare very favourably with those of the market. Below is a list of shops and stallholders selling especially good local food products.

There are far too many wine producers in this area of France to try and list any here, but see the relevant sections of the book for further information about places where you can visit cellars and taste the wine before buying – usually at a decent discount. Boulogne is also full of discount wine shops for booze cruisers.

Cheese
Fromagerie Germain is a specialist outlet for the powerful and smelly Langres cheese (*Rue de l'Aiguillon,*

Some French attitudes are worth embracing

Browse the delicatessens for culinary treats

Chalancey, 30km (19 miles) south of Langres. Tel: 03 25 84 84 03).

Fromagerie de Mussy is the place to buy the delicate, creamy, nutty-flavoured cow's cheese for which Chaource is renowned (*30 route de Maisons lès Chaource, Chaource, 30km (19 miles) south of Troyes. Tel: 03 25 73 24 35*).

Philippe Olivier Fromagerie is a very well-known cheese shop selling all sorts of different cheese but specialising in the local Maroilles (*3 rue Cure Saint-Étienne, Lille. Tel: 03 20 74 96 99*).

Cooked and cured meat
Boucherie du Forum sells *jambon de Reims*, a cooked ham seasoned with

champagne (*18 place Forum, Reims. Tel: 03 26 47 42 07*).

Charcuterie Demoizet is famed for its *boudin blanc* sausage and holds a sausage fest on the last Sunday in April each year (*1 rue Taine, Rethel (halfway between Charleville-Mézières and Reims). Tel: 03 24 38 42 05*).

Charcuterie Thierry Prautois specialises in *andouillette de Troyes* as well as a host of other charcuterie (*168 rue Général de Gaulle, Troyes. Tel: 03 25 73 06 46*).

Chez Mauricette offers all manner of charcuterie and cheese. Don't be put off by the queue – their *saucisson* is worth the wait (*Marché couvert, Place de la Cathédrale, Metz. Tel: 03 87 36 37 69*).

Kirn Traiteur is a top-quality and long-established butcher selling many Alsatian specialities (*19 rue du 22 Novembre, Strasbourg. Tel: 03 88 32 16 10*).

Drink

C Comme Champagne is an interesting champagne shop that gives you ample opportunity to taste various different champagne labels from small producers before you decide which to buy (*8 rue Gambetta, Épernay. Tel: 03 26 32 09 55*).

Sweets

La Cloche Lorraine specialises in the delicious madeleines for which the town is famous the world over, but also sells many other cakes and biscuits (*8 place Charles de Gaulle, Commercy, about 50km (31 miles) west of Nancy. Tel: 03 29 91 25 16*).

Markets

There are literally thousands of markets held throughout the region daily, weekly and monthly. For more details, contact the regional tourist boards (*see p153*):

Colmar local produce market (*Place de l'Ancienne. Open: Thur mornings*).

Lille flea market (*outside Église Saint-Pierre-et-Saint-Paul. Open: Sun*).

Lille Wazemmes market offers a huge spread of food, flowers, household products, and antiques and junk, and is one of the biggest general markets in France (*Place de la Nouvelle Aventure,*

Lille. Open: Tue, Thur & Sun 7am–2pm).

Metz flea market is the second-biggest flea market in France (*Expo, Rue de la Grange-aux-Bois, Metz. Tel: 03 87 55 66 00. Open: usually twice a month on Sat*).

Metz local produce market (*Place Saint-Jacques. Open: Tue, Thur & Sat mornings*).

Nancy flea market (*Grande Rue. Open: usually twice a month on Sun*).

Strasbourg farmers' market (*Place du Vieux Marché aux Poissons. Open: Sat mornings*).

Strasbourg flea market (*Rue de Vieil-Hôpital. Open: Wed & Sat mornings*).

Strasbourg local produce market (*in front of the Palais des Rohan. Open: Sat mornings*).

Christmas markets

Christmas is a big celebration in this part of the world and many of the region's cities (including Amiens, Charleville-Mézières, Colmar, Lille, Metz, Nancy, Reims, Strasbourg and Troyes) put on special Christmas fairs in their town centres. Glittering with lights and with the warming smell of *vin chaud* (mulled wine) in the air, they make an atmospheric run-up to the festive season as well as a good opportunity to buy some unusual gourmet, arts and crafty presents. The biggest of these markets are in Lille and Strasbourg. They usually start in the last week of November and carry on daily until 31 December.

Sport and leisure

With so much countryside to explore, northeast France is heaven if you are into outdoor sports. Its sandy beaches are a perfect backdrop for horse riding, its mountains attract cyclists, hikers and skiers all year round, its meandering rivers – well stocked with many breeds of fish – draw fishermen and canoeists from all over, and Champagne's sprawling reservoirs are multi-purpose watersports meccas.

Those who prefer more gentle pursuits – such as golf or thermal spas (*see below* and *p160*) – will not be disappointed and are also well provided for.
See also the 'Directory' section for listings of specific operators.

Cycling

Cycling and VTT (*vélo tout terrain*, or mountain biking) are hugely popular throughout France, and the northeast has more than its fair share of cycle-only paths and off-road tracks. All of the regional tourist board websites (*see p153*) can provide more specific information on cycle paths in their region, but the following are also useful sources of information about local routes, tours and cycle clubs.

Fédération Française de Cyclotourisme (*www.ffct.org*) has more general information about cycling clubs throughout France:

Ligue d'Alsace *4 rue Jean Mentelin, Strasbourg. Tel: 03 88 96 54 11. www.alsacecyclo.org*

Ligue Champagne-Ardenne *6 rue de l'Étang, Fontaine les Grés. About 20km (12½ miles) north of Troyes. Tel: 03 25 70 70 85. www.lca-ffct.org*

Ligue de Lorraine de Cyclotourisme *Château Salins. 30km (19 miles) northeast of Nancy. Tel: 03 87 05 10 76. http://lorraine.ffct.org*

Ligue Nord-Pas-de-Calais *367 rue Jules Guesde, Villeneuve d'Ascq. Tel: 03 20 05 68 05. www.ffct5962.com*

Ligue Picardy *2 rue des Vieilles-Écoles, Cauffry. 35km (22 miles) west of Compiègne. Tel: 03 44 73 28 28.*

Golf

Nord-Pas-de-Calais, Picardy and Lorraine are the best places to head for if you want to play golf. The north coast has some wonderful courses looking out to sea. The *Golf Today* website (*www.golftoday.co.uk*) is a very useful source of detailed information about courses throughout the country, broken down into regions and *départements*. Below are a few particularly good and beautifully situated courses that are open to non-members. Booking is advised, however:

Golf d'Amnéville-les-Thermes *Centre Thermal et Touristique, Amnéville-les-Thermes. Tel: 03 87 71 30 13. www.golf-amneville.com*

Golf de Belle Dune *Promenade du Marquenterre, Fort-Mahon-Plage. Tel: 03 22 23 45 50.*

Golf de Compiègne *Avenue Royale, Compiègne. Tel: 03 44 38 48 00. www.golf-compiegne.com*

Golf de Nampont Saint-Martin *Maison Forte, Nampont Saint-Martin. Tel: 03 22 29 92 90. www.nampontgolfclub.com*

Golf de Reims-Champagne *Château des Dames de France, Gueux. Tel: 03 26 05 46 10. www.golf-de-reims.com*

Hiking

There are thousands of kilometres of Grande and Petite Randonnée (GR and PR) trails throughout the region, ranging from little more than gentle strolls along the cliffs south of Calais through to hikes up the highest peaks of the Vosges. If you want to follow either a GR or a PR trail, you are advised to get either the relevant map from the **Fédération française de la randonnée Pédestre** (*www.ffrandonnee.fr*)or the large-scale, Ordnance Survey-type

Hiking is a great way to experience the region's lesser-known gems

maps published by the **Institut Géographique National** (*www.ign.fr*). These latter are available in England at **Stanfords** travel bookshops in London and Bristol (*www.stanfords.co.uk*), if you wish to purchase them before you travel. The GR and PR trails are also fairly well signposted along the routes. The **Club Vosgien** (*www.club-vosgien.eu*) is another very useful source of information about climbing in the Vosges.

Horse riding

Again, there are thousands of miles of bridle paths all over France. It's particularly popular around the Baie de la Somme where you can ride the local Henson breed along the endless flat sandy bay (*see p174*). For vast amounts of useful information on bridle paths and stables across the region, see the **Comité National de Tourisme Équestre** website, *www.cnte.fr*

Skiing

Spread across Lorraine and Alsace, the Vosges mountains may not be as high as the Alps – the highest point is only about 1,400m (4,595ft) – but there are still plenty of ski resorts here to test even the most hardened skier – as well as some of the best cross-country skiing in France.

The bigger resorts for alpine skiing in this part of France include **La Bresse** (*www.labresse.labellemontagne.com*), **Gérardmer** (*www.gerardmer-ski.com*), **Le Lac Blanc** (*www.lac-blanc.com*),

Le Markstein and **Le Grand Ballon** (*www.lemarkstein.net*) and **Le Schnepfenried** (*www.leschnepf.com*). They are all pretty small compared to Alpine resorts, but you should have enough runs at each of them to keep you occupied for at least half a day, and there are hotels and chalets available if you want to stay in the mountains. For cross-country or nordic skiing, head for **Schneeberg** (*www.suisse-alsace.com*), **Donon** (*www.hautebruche.com*), **Champ de Feu** (*www.lechampdefeu.com*) and **Les Bagenelles** (*www.lesbagenelles.com*).

For a good source of general information about skiing in France, visit *www.pistehors.com*

Spas

The thermal spas of the Lorraine Vosges (*see pp104–5*) were once world-renowned medical centres with people travelling from all over Europe to 'take the waters' here. Places like Vittel, Bains-les-Bains, Contrexéville and Plombières-les-Bains are still viewed by many to have therapeutic effects and attract a lot of health tourism, but you can find spas for mere relaxation, well-being and beauty treatments here too. The Vosges *département* tourist board website (*www.tourismevosges.fr*) has plenty of information.

Watersports

There is a huge amount of variety when it comes to choice of watersports: fishing, kayaking, diving, windsurfing and sailing are all possible, either in the sea or in the region's many rivers and lakes.

Fishing

For information about fishing in the region, contact the **Fédération de Pêche** (*www.unpf.fr*). You will need to get a permit (available from fishing shops and bar-tabacs, cafés that also sell cigarettes, stamps, etc.) – day and holiday (in summer) permits are available.

Kayaking and canoeing

The different rivers of the region present a variety of options for kayaking and canoeing, from gently drifting down the Meuse and the Marne to something a bit more lively on one of their tributaries like the Blaise or the Saulx. The **Fédération Française de Canoe-Kayak** (*www.ffck.org*) can help with maps and local club information.

Windsurfing and sailing

Windsurfing, sailing and even scuba diving are all possible on the Lac d'Orient, part of the **Parc Naturel Régional de la Forêt d'Orient** (*www.pnr-foret-orient.fr*) in Champagne. (The other two lakes in the park, Lac du Temple and Lac Amance, are reserved for canoeists and water skiing, respectively.) There's also a marina on the **Lac du Der-Chantecoq** (*www.lacduder.com*), one of the biggest lakes in Europe. Sailing is also of course possible in the Channel, and there are several marinas along the coast south of Calais. For further general information, check out the **France Station Nautique** website, *www.station-nautique.com*

Cyclists on the Route du Vin

Sport and leisure

Children

It's unlikely that you will be stuck for ideas when it comes to entertaining your children in this part of the world. As well as the fuss that is likely to be made of them (especially younger kids) wherever you go, there are plenty of theme and adventure parks, fairy-tale castles, sandy beaches and hundreds of other outdoor activities (see 'Sport and leisure') to keep them occupied.

Older children, perhaps boys especially, will almost certainly be fascinated by the fortifications from World War I and World War II.

Practicalities

Most hotels will arrange for an extra bed to be put in your room for a small charge, if necessary, and they usually offer babysitting services too (although it is worth checking before you book). Children are welcomed in bars and restaurants at any time of day or night but one of the advantages of eating out in France is that meal times are generally earlier than they are in Britain. It is perfectly possible to eat at 7–7.30pm in most restaurants. Many places also have special children's menus.

Sights and activities
Château Fleckenstein

A spectacularly situated ruin of a castle perched on a hill in the northern Vosges, right on the border with

Germany, the ruin itself is a fascinating place for children to visit and let their imagination run riot, but there are also many other fun medieval knight- and princess-themed activities such as Le Château des Défis (the Castle of Challenges) and Le P'tit Fleck adventure playground.
Lembach. Tel: 03 88 94 28 52. www.fleckenstein.fr. Open: Apr–Jun, Sept & Oct 10am–6pm; Jul & Aug 10am–6.30pm; early Nov 10am–5pm. Ticket office closes two and a half hours before closing time. Admission charge.

Christmas

Christmas is a great time to bring children to northeast France. The Christmas markets (*see p157*) all have children's activities and, of course, Santa Claus in attendance. If you are planning to come around this time of year, try and time your visit for the Fête de Saint-Nicolas (Feast of St Nicholas) on 6 December. Many towns across the region have torch-lit processions, fireworks and parades.

Parc Animalier de Sainte-Croix

This is a wildlife park covering an impressive 120 hectares (295 acres) in the countryside of east Lorraine. As well as seeing hundreds of different species of mammal, such as Arctic and European wolves, brown bears, raccoons, lynxes and American bison, it is also possible to stay overnight in the park in a 'trappers' cabin or, if you are really brave, to bivouac under canvas.

Rhodes, 60km (37 miles) east of Nancy. Tel: 03 87 03 92 05. www.parcsainte croix.com. Open: Apr–Jun, Sept & Oct 10am–6pm; Jul & Aug 10am–7pm. Admission charge, and extra charges if you are staying overnight.

Puppet shows

These are popular in this part of the world and Charleville-Mézières is an important centre of puppetry: its international festival is held every three years – the next is in 2012. The **Musée des Marionnettes du Monde** has information about forthcoming puppetry events and small festivals as well as an exhibition of puppets from around the world (*Buire le Sec, 60km (37 miles) south of Boulogne-sur-Mer. Tel: 03 21 81 80 34. marionnettes-du-monde.com*).

For further information on puppet shows, ask at the local or regional tourist office.

Walygator Parc

This alligator-inspired theme park, which is about 15km (9¼ miles) north of Metz, has around 60 different rides and attractions, including Europe's largest inverted roller coaster.

Voie Romaine, Maizières-lès-Metz. Tel: 03 87 30 70 07. www.walygator parc.com. Open: mid-Apr–end Apr daily 11am–6pm; May, Jun, Sept & Oct Sat & Sun 11am–6pm; Jul & Aug daily 10.30am–6.30pm; check website for further details of opening times. Admission charge.

Charleville-Mézière's marionnette clock

Essentials

Arriving and departing
By air
The main international airport for the region is Paris-Charles de Gaulle (CDG) (*www.aeroportsdeparis.fr*), which has direct flights from most European cities and from many US and Asian cities too. All the major cities of the northeast region are less than three hours by TGV (Train de Grande Vitesse, high-speed train) from Paris Gare de L'Est. There are a few flights to Strasbourg from Paris, but the TGV, which serves the airport station, may well be a more convenient option.

By sea
Calais and Dunkerque are the main ports of entry on the north coast. They are served by **Norfolk Line** (*Tel: 0871 574 7235. www.norfolkline.com*), **P&O Ferries** (*Tel: 0871 664 2121. www.poferries.com*) and **Sea France** (*Tel: 0871 423 7119. www.seafrance. com*) from Dover only.

By rail
The **Eurostar** (*Tel: 0843 218 6186. www.eurostar.com*) from St Pancras International in London to Lille Europe is the quickest way to reach northeast France. The journey takes about an hour and a half. From Lille (Europe or Flandres stations), there are TGV and other rail connections to towns throughout the region with **SNCF** (*www.voyages-sncf.com*). There is also a car-rail service to Calais from Folkestone with **Eurotunnel** (*Tel: 0844 335 3535. www.eurotunnel.com*) – the crossing under the Channel takes about 30 minutes. From Calais, there are good motorway connections to the rest of northeast France.

Customs
If you are travelling from France to another EU country (or the other way round), you can bring in as much of any legal substance as you like, as long as it is for personal use. Visitors from outside the EU can bring in a litre of spirits, 4 litres of wine, 16 litres of beer and 200 cigarettes (50 cigars or 250

Try out your French at tourist information centres

grams of rolling tobacco). Check with your home country's customs authorities to find out how much you can bring back from France.

Electricity

The electricity supply in France is AC 220/240 volts, 50 Hertz. Plugs have two round pins. Adaptors are readily available at stations, airports and other ports of entry.

Internet

You will find Internet cafés in towns and cities across the region, and most hotels and B&Bs will supply Wi-Fi or a direct plug-in connection (sometimes this is free, but not always). Wi-Fi is also increasingly common in cafés and bars.

Money

The official currency is the euro, which is divided into 100 euro cents (called *centimes* in France). Notes come in the following denominations: 5, 10, 20, 50, 100, 200, 500; and coins as 1, 2, 5, 10, 20, 50 cents, and 1 and 2 euros. Almost all bank ATMs accept the vast majority of debit and credit cards these days, so getting hold of money is not usually a problem, although you may have to pay a foreign transaction fee – as well as possibly being hit with an unfavourable exchange rate. ATMs are ubiquitous in all towns and cities. Paying with a credit or debit card is very common now, but don't bank on it. If in doubt, check with a hotel or restaurant when booking.

CONVERSION TABLE

FROM	TO	MULTIPLY BY
Inches	Centimetres	2.54
Feet	Metres	0.3048
Yards	Metres	0.9144
Miles	Kilometres	1.6090
Acres	Hectares	0.4047
Gallons	Litres	4.5460
Ounces	Grams	28.35
Pounds	Grams	453.6
Pounds	Kilograms	0.4536
Tons	Tonnes	1.0160

To convert back, for example from centimetres to inches, divide by the number in the third column.

MEN'S SUITS

UK	36	38	40	42	44	46	48
Rest of Europe	46	48	50	52	54	56	58
USA	36	38	40	42	44	46	48

DRESS SIZES

UK	8	10	12	14	16	18
France	36	38	40	42	44	46
Italy	38	40	42	44	46	48
Rest of Europe	34	36	38	40	42	44
USA	6	8	10	12	14	16

MEN'S SHIRTS

UK	14	14.5	15	15.5	16	16.5	17
Rest of Europe	36	37	38	39/40	41	42	43
USA	14	14.5	15	15.5	16	16.5	17

MEN'S SHOES

UK	7	7.5	8.5	9.5	10.5	11
Rest of Europe	41	42	43	44	45	46
USA	8	8.5	9.5	10.5	11.5	12

WOMEN'S SHOES

UK	4.5	5	5.5	6	6.5	7
Rest of Europe	38	38	39	39	40	41
USA	6	6.5	7	7.5	8	8.5

Opening hours

Most shops are open Mon–Sat 9am–noon and 2–7pm. The two-hour lunch break is not universal, but don't be surprised if you find places closed at this time of day. Larger department stores are usually open 9am–7pm, and big out-of-town supermarkets often open from 8am–8pm. Sunday closing is still pretty much the norm. Bank opening hours are usually Tue–Sat 10am–1pm and 3–5pm. Opening times for sights and museums vary considerably.

Passports and visas

EU citizens do not require a visa to enter France; a valid passport is sufficient. Visitors from the US, Canada, Australia and New Zealand are entitled to stay for up to 90 days without a visa. A short-stay visa is necessary for South African citizens.

Pharmacies

Pharmacies, clearly marked by a big green cross, are widely available in towns and cities across the region. Note that most are not open on Sundays but they will have information posted up with the details of the nearest 24-hour pharmacy.

Post

La Poste is the French postal service. Post boxes are yellow and have either 'La Poste' or 'Postes' written on them. Stamps are available in *bar-tabacs* (cafés that also sell cigarettes, etc.).

Public holidays

1 January – Jour de l'An (New Year's Day)

March/April – Pâques (Easter Sunday and Monday)

1 May – Fête du Travail (May Day/ Labour Day)

8 May – Victoire 1945 (VE Day)

40th day after Easter – L'Ascension (Ascension Day)

7th Sunday after Easter – Pentecôte (Whit Sunday and Monday)

14 July – Fête Nationale (Bastille Day)

15 August – L'Assomption (Assumption)

1 November – La Toussaint (All Saints' Day)

11 November – Jour d'Armistice (Remembrance Day)

25 December – Noël (Christmas Day)

Smoking

Smoking anywhere indoors is prohibited in France and this law is generally adhered to. However, you will find that many restaurants have heated outdoor covered areas where smoking is permissible.

Suggested reading and media

1914–1918: The History of the First World War (2005) is a clear and highly regarded overview of the conflict by David Stevenson.

A Hilltop on the Marne (1915) is a collection of letters written by Englishwoman Mildred Aldrich, caught up in the fighting of World War I.

*Maginot Line 1940: Battles on the French

Frontier (2010), written by Marc Romanych and Martin Rupp, gives an interesting account of the German operations against the French defences. *The Pâtissier: Recipes and Conversations from Alsace* (2006) is a cookbook and diary of a new life in Strasbourg by Susan Lundquist, Hossine Bennara and Frederic Lacroix.

The Reluctant Tommy: An Extraordinary Memoir of the First World War (2010) is a memoir by Ronald Skirth, a British private serving in French Flanders during World War I. It is an especially interesting account of the war, given that it is one of very few written by someone of this rank.

Tax

A TVA (VAT) tax of 19.6 per cent is added to most purchases in France. If you live outside the EU, you can recoup some of this on purchases over €175. Keep receipts and forms filled out in the shop to show customs on departure.

Telephones

Most public telephones in France operate with a *télécarte* (obtainable at newsagents and *tabacs*) but the prevalence of mobile phones and reduced roaming rates means that you are more likely to use your mobile. It is also possible to buy sim cards in France to avoid roaming charges. The country code for France is +33, and the area code for northeast France is 03. Mobile numbers start with 06. Numbers beginning with 08 are premium-rate national numbers.

Time

France is on Central European Time (CET, one hour ahead of GMT) in winter and CET+1 in summer.

Toilets

Public toilets are common in French towns and are usually coin-operated and automatically cleaned.

Travellers with disabilities

Disabled facilities are improving rapidly in France, with ramp access and parking spaces for disabled people now common in all towns across the region. Most hotels will have rooms specially kitted out, and almost all museums and sights will have wheelchair access.

Take time to enjoy Alsace's cuisine

Language

Making the effort to use what French you have will reap rewards when it comes to communicating with people in France even if (as is quite possible) they then reply to you in perfect English. You will find that English is widely spoken throughout the region in touristy areas, shops and especially at important sights where English-speaking guides are often available. However, in other places, such as small villages and away from the beaten tourist track, do not assume that people will know any English at all.

Pronunciation
Vowels

a as in 'cat'; **ar** as in 'hard'; **an** as in 'long'; **ae** as in 'aeroplane'; **ai** as in 'hay'; **au** like the 'o' in 'hope'

e as in 'kept' if it comes at the beginning of the word or 'lurk' if it comes after a consonant; **er** as in 'lair' or 'hay' if it comes at the end of the word; **eu** as in 'lurk'; **eau** as in 'hope'

i as in 'keep'

o as in 'hop'; **oi** as in 'swag'; **ou** as in 'hoop', **oui** as in 'weed'

u and 'too'

Silent consonants

Consonants at the end of words are usually silent, as is **h** in almost all cases and **n** if it comes after a vowel.

BASIC WORDS AND PHRASES

yes	oui	**I have**	j'ai
no	non	**it is . . .**	c'est
please	s'il vous plaît	**Do you speak**	Parlez-vous
thank you	merci	**English?**	anglais?
excuse me	pardon	**I do not**	Je ne
I am sorry	pardon	**understand**	comprends pas
good morning	bonjour	**a little**	un peu
good evening	bonsoir	**much/many**	beaucoup
good night	bonne nuit	**enough**	assez
goodbye	au revoir	**too much/many**	trop

DAYS OF THE WEEK

Monday	lundi
Tuesday	mardi
Wednesday	mercredi
Thursday	jeudi
Friday	vendredi
Saturday	samedi
Sunday	dimanche

MONTHS

January	janvier
February	février
March	mars
April	avril
May	mai
June	juin
July	juillet
August	août
September	septembre
October	octobre
November	novembre
December	décembre

NUMBERS

0	zéro	18	dix-huit
1	un, une	19	dix-neuf
2	deux	20	vingt
3	trois	21	vingt et un
4	quatre	22	vingt-deux
5	cinq	30	trente
6	six	40	quarante
7	sept	50	cinquante
8	huit	60	soixante
9	neuf	70	soixante-dix
10	dix	80	quatre-vingts
11	onze	90	quatre-vingt-dix
12	douze	100	cent
13	treize	200	deux cents
14	quatorze	300	trois cents
15	quinze	1,000	mille
16	seize	2,000	deux mille
17	dix-sept	1,000,000	un million

OTHER PHRASES

when	quand
yesterday	hier
today	aujourd'hui
tomorrow	demain
at what time . . .?	à quelle heure . . .?
where is . . .?	où est . . .?
here	ici
there	là
near	près
before	avant
in front of	devant
behind	derrière
opposite	en face de
right	à droite
left	à gauche
straight on	tout droit
car park	un parking
petrol station	une station-service
parking	stationnement
prohibited	interdit
bridge	le pont
street	la rue

bus stop	l'arrêt du bus
railway station	la gare
platform	le quai
ticket	un billet
ten métro tickets	un carnet
single ticket	un aller simple
Have you got a table?	Avez-vous une table libre?
I want to reserve a table	Je voudrais réserver une table
I am a vegetarian	Je suis végétarian
I'm having the €20 set menu	Je prendrai le menu à vingt euros
The bill please	L'addition s'il vous plaît
How do you say... (in French)	Comment dites-vous... (en français)
Can you speak slower, please?	Parlez moins vite, s'il vous plaît.
Can you repeat please?	Pouvez-vous répéter, s'il vous plaît.
Help!	Au secours!
Wait!	Attendez!
Stop!	Arrêtez!

Emergencies

Emergency numbers

For all emergencies, call *112*.
This is the number to call for police, fire and ambulance and also for details of your nearest 24-hour pharmacy.

Health risks

There are no major health risks associated with being in northeast France – except perhaps for annoying mosquito bites, so remember to bring insect repellant if you're visiting in summer. It is generally safe to drink tap water all over France, except when it is specifically labelled 'eau non potable'. In cafés and restaurants you will often be given – or can request – *une carafe d'eau* (a jug of water), which is free for the table and is perfectly safe to drink.

Medical services

You will find at least one doctor's surgery in all towns no matter how small they are. It's worth asking locals (or at the local pharmacy) for a recommendation; failing that, details of local doctors (*médecins*) and hospitals (*centres hospitaliers*) with accident and emergency units (*l'urgence*) are listed in yellow pages and online at *www.pagesjaunes.fr*

Outside normal working hours, medical assistance can be summoned from **SOS Médecins** (*www.sosmedecins-france.fr*), who will come to your house or hotel.

Insurance

EU citizens are entitled to a certain amount of free healthcare if they are in possession of a European Health Insurance Card (EHIC). UK citizens can apply for one online at *www.ehic.org.uk* or at their local post office. If possible, make sure that you give this to the doctor before treatment begins, and be prepared for some paperwork. Note that this does not cover emergency dental treatment, treatment from opticians or repatriation, so you are strongly advised to take out travel insurance that will cover these as well. Non-EU citizens are not covered by reciprocal health agreements with France so should always travel with insurance that covers all medical treatment – and make sure it covers dangerous sports like skiing. Insurance is generally cheap and will cover you for vital repatriation if necessary as well as for theft and loss of belongings.

Safety and crime
Crime

Crime (both petty and violent) is generally speaking very low in northeast France. That said, walking alone down dark streets in big cities like Lille is obviously not advised, as elsewhere in the world, and you should always be aware of pickpockets in crowded places like markets. Otherwise, however, you should feel very safe. Most hotels have safes for rent if you want to leave your valuables locked up, and always remember to lock your car. To report a crime, either call the emergency number (*112* – but only in an emergency!) or go to the local *commissariat de police* (police station) with your passport. Report any loss or theft immediately to the police, if only for insurance purposes.

Police

There are several different police forces in France: the Police Nationale (dealing with local crimes within towns), the Gendarmerie Nationale (working on a national level and enforcing traffic laws) and the notorious Compagnie Républicaine de la Sécurité (known as the riot police) are all national forces and are armed. The Police Municipal deals with local petty crime. You may also see the *douanes* police force (responsible for customs) on the motorways and in border areas. If you are ever stopped while you are driving, you will be expected to provide your passport and car documents.

Embassies and consulates

Australian Embassy *4 rue Jean Rey, Paris. Tel: 01 40 59 33 00.*
www.france.embassy.gov.au

Canadian Embassy *35 avenue Montaigne, Paris. Tel: 01 44 43 29 02.*
www.canadainternational.gc.ca
Irish Embassy *12 avenue Foch, Paris. Tel: 01 44 17 67 00.*
www.embassyofireland.fr
New Zealand Embassy *7ter rue Léonard de Vinci, Paris. Tel: 01 45 01 43 43.*
www.nzembassy.com/france
UK Embassy *35 rue du Faubourg Saint-Honoré, Paris. Tel: 01 44 51 31 00.*
http://ukinfrance.fco.gov.uk
US Consulate *15 avenue d'Alsace, Strasbourg. Tel: 03 88 35 31 04.*
http://strasbourg.usconsulate.gov
US Embassy *2 avenue Gabriel, Paris. Tel: 01 43 12 22 22.*
http://france.usembassy.gov

Emergencies

Most towns have a 24-hour pharmacy

Directory

Accommodation price guide

The prices are based on the cost of a double room.

£	under €60
££	€60–100
£££	€100–150
££££	over €150

Eating out price guide

The prices are based on the cost of a two-course meal for one person. Note that opening hours have been given in general terms (i.e. 'lunch' and 'dinner') for some places where precise hours were not available. This should roughly correspond to noon–2pm and 7.30–9.30pm. Many restaurants are closed for all or part of August and sometimes at other holiday times too.

£	under €25
££	€25–35
£££	€35–50
££££	over €50

THE NORTH

Lille

ACCOMMODATION

L'Hermitage Gantois ££££

One of Lille's most expensive hotels (but with a very reasonable brasserie), the Hermitage is a gorgeous, restored 14th-century monastery a short walk away from the station and the Palais des Beaux-Arts. However, note that some of the rooms may not live up to the standard of the splendid lobby and courtyard areas (ask to see them first if possible).

224 rue de Paris. Tel: 03 20 85 30 30. www. hotelhermitagegantois.com

EATING OUT

Les 3 Brasseurs £

There's a warm beery smell to this brasserie that serves hearty bistro and brasserie fare and brews its own ale on site. Most people come here for the beer rather than to eat.

22 place de la Gare. Tel: 03 20 06 46 25. www.les3brasseurs.com. Open: daily until late.

Brasserie de la Paix ££

Another Lillois institution, this is a perfect lunch or evening venue in the heart of the city, serving classic brasserie dishes, especially mussels.

25 place Rihour. Tel: 03 20 54 70 41. Open: Mon–Sat noon–2.30pm & 7–11.30pm.

À L'Huîtrière ££££

A local legend, this one-time fishmongers has been serving up delectable seafood since 1928 and is still run by the same family. Turbot and crêpes Suzette are two of the restaurant's specialities. One of four

Michelin-starred restaurants in Lille.
3 rue des Chats Bossus.
Tel: 03 20 55 43 41.
www.huitriere.fr.
Closed: Sun dinner,
public holidays dinner &
most of August.

Centre Chorégraphique National Roubaix Nord-Pas-de-Calais

The internationally acclaimed Ballet du Nord is based in Roubaix near Lille and has a richly varied programme of mainly contemporary dance performances.
33 rue de l'Epeule, Roubaix.
Tel: 03 20 24 66 66.
www.ccn-roubaix.com

Cinema Le Majestic

Arts cinema that shows some films in their original language (with French subtitles) and is the venue for various local film festivals.
54–56 rue de Béthune.
Tel: 03 28 52 40 40.
www.lemajesticlille.com

Network Café

One of Lille's most popular nightclubs playing an eclectic mix of dance music, rock,

salsa, hip hop, etc.
15 rue du Faisan. Tel: 03 20 40 04 91.
www.networkcafe.fr.
Open: daily 10.30pm until late.

Opéra de Lille

Lille's grand theatre and opera house (on Place du Théâtre in the centre of the city) has cutting-edge opera, dance and classical concerts as well as more mainstream classical performances of works by the likes of Mozart and Donizetti. Check the website for details of what's on.
2 rue des Bons Enfants.
Tel: (08) 20 48 90 00.
www.opera-lille.fr

Orchestre Nationale de Lille

This highly regarded regional orchestra with a firm local following sometimes attracts international soloists. Check the website for details of their varied programme.
3 place Mendès. Tel: 03 20 12 82 40. www.onlille.com

Sapo

A sophisticated place for a cocktail on a trendy street, Le Sapo is a

popular lounge bar-club at which to start the evening off.
11 rue de Gand. Tel: 03 20 74 31 16.

Ch'ti velo

Cycle hire in Lille. A deposit of €300 and identification are required.
10 avenue Willy Brandt.
Tel: 03 28 53 07 49.
www.chti-velo.fr

Nord-Pas-de-Calais

La Chatellerie du Schoebeque £££–££££

There is a varied selection of individually styled rooms and suites at this 18th-century house in Cassel overlooking the rolling Flanders countryside – from the frou-frou *La Vie en Rose* or *Pompadour* to the exotic *La City of Africa*. There's also a spa centre – see the website for various well-being packages – and a swimming pool.
32 rue du Maréchal Foch, Cassel.
Tel: 03 28 42 42 67.
www.schoebeque.com

Côte d'Opale

ACCOMMODATION

Du Port et des Bains £–££

Welcoming little hotel with 16 simple, small but neatly decorated rooms overlooking Saint-Valéry-sur-Somme's harbour and the Somme estuary. Also has an excellent and highly regarded seafood restaurant attached, so the place is usually buzzing in summer.
1 quai Balvet, Saint-Valéry-sur-Somme.
Tel: 03 22 60 80 09.
www.hotelhpb.com

La Longue Roye £–££

A charming B&B with just five simply decorated rooms in a former Cistercian monastery and farm dating from the 13th century. The hamlet of Longvilliers is 10km (6¼ miles) east of Le Touquet and 25km (15½ miles) south of Boulogne.
62630 Longvilliers.
Tel: 03 21 86 70 65.

Château de Montreuil ££££

This luxury hotel outside Montreuil-sur-Mer is set in a very pretty garden and has an elegant, country-house style. One of the best (and certainly one of the most expensive) places to stay in the region. The restaurant has a Michelin star.
4 chaussée des Capucins, Montreuil-sur-Mer.
Tel: 03 21 81 53 04.
www.chateaudemontreuil. com

EATING OUT

Du Port et des Bains £–££

Bright and cheery little harbourside restaurant (and hotel, *see p40*) serving up excellent simple, fresh seafood to tourists and locals alike. Usually pretty busy in summer.
Located at 'Du Port et des Bains' above. Open: daily. Closed: mid-Nov–early Dec & most of Jan.

SPORT AND LEISURE

Centre Équestre du Vimeu

This centre can organise horse-riding trips in the beautiful sweeping landscape of the Somme bay area.
51 rue Marius Briet, Friville Escarbotin, 20km (12½ miles) south of Saint-Valéry-sur-Somme. Tel: 03 22 30 29 36. www. centreequestreduvimeu.fr

Arras and the Somme

ACCOMMODATION

La Corne d'Or ££–£££

An elegant B&B in the centre of Arras in an 18th-century house, La Corne d'Or has five attractively decorated bedrooms, all with their own classical-contemporary style and with varying degrees of luxury and price. One of the rooms, in the attic of the house, even has World War I shrapnel in its wooden beams and views over the rooftops of Arras.
1 place Guy-Mollet, Arras. Tel: 03 21 58 85 94. www.lamaisondhotes.com. Closed: usually mid-Jul–mid-Aug.

La Chartreuse du Val Saint-Esprit £££–££££

A large hotel with 53 rooms in a beautiful 18th-century manor house set around a courtyard and attractive grounds. All bedrooms are elegantly and individually furnished, and the restaurants, all

three of them, serve good (though expensive) regional cuisine with an impressive wine list.
1 rue des Fouquières, Gosnay, near the town of Bethune and 35km (22 miles) north of Arras. Tel: 03 21 62 80 00. www.lachartreuse.com

EATING OUT
Le Carpe Diem £
A brasserie that's popular with locals and visitors alike, Le Carpe Diem specialises in the city's favourite sausage, *andouillette*, as well as other regional dishes such as chicken cooked in cream, and *maroilles*, a strong local cheese. Reservation strongly recommended.
8 rue des Petits Viéziers, Arras. Tel: 03 21 51 70 08. Closed: Mon dinner & Sun (but open Sun lunch in summer).

SPORT AND LEISURE
Stade d'Eau Vive – Base Nautique
Kayaking, canoeing and white-water rafting are possible at these artificial river rapids.
Rue Laurent Gers, Saint-Laurent-Blangy, 2km (1¼ miles) northeast of Arras. Tel: 03 21 73 74 93. Open: daily 9am–5pm, but call to make a reservation first.

Douai to Cambrai
EATING OUT
Auberge Fontenoise
£££–££££
You'll find top-quality regional and traditional fare at this family-run *auberge* 4km (2½ miles) outside Cambrai on the road heading west to Bapaume. A father-and-son chef team bring regional specialities, more traditional French favourites and a dash of international flare to the table.
543 route de Bapaume, Fontaine-Notre-Dame. Tel: 03 27 37 71 24. www.auberge-fontenoise.com. Open: Tue–Sun lunch.

Amiens to Beauvais
ACCOMMODATION
All Seasons Cathédrale
££–£££
Comfortable and well-appointed chain hotel in a lovely 18th-century post house in the centre of Amiens. The simple rooms are bright and contemporary in style and the hotel has all the amenities you'd expect of a 3-star hotel, including a bar.
17–19 place au Feurre, Amiens. Tel: 03 22 22 00 20. www.allseasons.com

EATING OUT
La Queue de Vache £
On trendy Quai Bélu in the Saint-Leu quarter of Amiens, this busy wine bar-cum-restaurant serves simple dishes (like charcuterie and cheese platters) in a cosy atmosphere. There is also an outdoor terrace that overlooks the Somme river and weekly live jazz gigs (usually on Tuesdays, but ring to check). The name means 'The Cow's Tail'.
51 quai Bélu, Amiens. Tel: 03 22 91 38 91. Open: Mon–Sat noon–2pm & 7–10pm, Sun noon–2pm.
Au Relais des Orfèvres £££
A great place to sample excellent local cuisine very near the cathedral in Amiens. The various differently priced menus

(including a tasting menu) provide an opportunity to sample regional favourites and standard classics from talented chef Jean-Michel Descloux.

14 rue des Orfèvres, Amiens. Tel: 03 22 92 36 01. www.restaurant-relais-orfevres.fr. Open: Tue–Fri lunch & dinner, Sat dinner. Closed: Sat lunch, Sun, most of Aug & often Feb.

SPORT AND LEISURE
Golf de Saint-Quentin-Mesnil

Renowned and well-established golf course in a region that is well known for having some of the best golf courses in Europe. Reservation required.

Rue du Chêne de Cambrie, Mesnil-Saint-Laurent, 6km (3¾ miles) east of Saint-Quentin. Tel: 03 23 68 19 48. www.golf-saint-quentin.org

Compiègne and surrounds
ACCOMMODATION
L'Ermitage £–££

Lovely and very good-value *chambre d'hôte* in a 19th-century manor house just outside Pierrefonds in the Forêt de Compiègne with views from its spacious and elegantly decorated rooms that stretch out across cow pastures to the trees beyond. Offers an excellent breakfast too.

74 rue Impératrice Eugénie, Pierrefonds. Tel: 03 44 42 85 64. www.ermitage-pierrefonds.fr

Hôtel Belle Vue £–££

An old-fashioned hotel within the castle walls of Coucy-le-Château, and the only choice in town. Some of the basic, and slightly down-at-heel, rooms have splendidly atmospheric views of the castle and town walls. The restaurant serves traditional Picardy dishes in a dark wooden dining room with views over the town, or on a pleasant shady terrace.

Upper Town, Coucy-le-Château-Auffrique. Tel: 03 23 52 69 70. www.hotel-bellevue-coucy.com

EATING OUT
Le Bistrot des Arts £–££

A classic-looking, dark and cosy little bistro in Compiègne's Hôtel des Beaux-Arts. With its walls covered in old posters, it serves simple, fresh seasonal dishes in a friendly and relaxed environment.

33 cours Guynemer, Compiègne. Tel: 03 44 20 10 10. Open: Mon–Fri noon–2pm & 7–10pm, Sat 7–10pm.

Chez Raphaël ££

Great-quality and good-value food is served in simple, pleasant surroundings at this bistro-style place near the banks of the Ainse river in the centre of Soissons. Expect a warm welcome from patron and chef Raphaël.

7 rue Saint-Quentin, Soissons. Tel: 03 23 93 51 79. Open: Mon–Fri lunch & dinner, Sat dinner only, Sun lunch only. Closed: Mon.

Auberge de Daguet £££

A very traditional, even old-fashioned, French restaurant in a pretty little village in the heart of the Forêt de Compiègne. The huge fireplace, wooden beams and tapestried chairs set the scene for some excellent dishes such as chicken breast stuffed with ground veal and lardons (bacon cubes). *Opposite the church, Vieux Moulin, 10km (6¼ miles) east of Compiègne. Tel: 03 44 85 60 72. www.auberge.du.daguet. free.fr. Open: Wed–Sun lunch & dinner. Closed: public holidays.*

CHAMPAGNE-ARDENNE

Reims

ACCOMMODATION

Le Cheval Blanc ££–£££

A friendly, quiet and family-run hotel easily accessible (about 30 minutes by car on the A4 autoroute) from the centre of Reims in the village of Sept-Saulx. The hotel is set in large grounds with the river Vesle running though the garden. The cheaper rooms are quite a bit smaller than the more expensive ones, but the hotel also offers various half-board packages which include good-quality and good-value meals in its restaurant.

Rue du Moulin, Sept-Saulx, 25km (15½ miles) southeast of Reims. Tel: 03 26 03 90 27. www.chevalblanc-sept-saulx.com

Grand Hôtel de l'Univers ££–£££

Comfortable and good-value rooms in a characterful Art Deco building a short walk from the centre of Reims, overlooking the smart 18th-century Hautes Promenades and Place Colbert. Convenient for the train station, all rooms are double-glazed so noise should not be a problem. The hotel also has a smart lounge-bar and a restaurant. *41 boulevard Foch. Tel: 03 26 88 68 08. www. hotel-univers-reims.com*

Domaine Ployez-Jacquemart £££

Ployez-Jacquemart offers a rare opportunity to stay at a working champagne house. The five rooms at this B&B in a 19th-century country mansion are all elegant and well equipped, and the house is surrounded by the Pinot Noir and Pinot Meunier vineyards of the Premier and Grand Cru villages of Ludes and Mailly-Champagne. As well as offering exceptional and friendly hospitality in the form of accommodation, you can also dine here (if you book in advance) and sample the various vintage champagnes made by the house and stored in vast cellars underneath the building. *8 rue Astoin, Ludes, 15km (9¼ miles) south of Reims. Tel: 03 26 61 11 87. www.ployez-jacquemart.fr*

L'Assiette Champenoise £££–££££

Set in its own large park about 3km (1¾ miles) from the centre of Reims in the suburb of Tinqueux, this *fin de siècle* 'château' hotel has a variety of different rooms (55 in total) ranging in price and luxury. All have been recently smartly decorated in contemporary styles and colours. The hotel really shines, though, in its two-Michelin-starred restaurant overlooking the park that serves exquisitely prepared traditional French cuisine and, as you would expect, offers a well-stocked cellar.

40 avenue Paul Vaillant-Couturier. Tel: 03 26 84 64 64. www. assiettechampenoise.com

EATING OUT

La Brasserie du Boulingrin ££

A splendidly authentic and bustling French brasserie a few minutes' walk north of the cathedral in central Reims.

48 rue de Mars. Tel: 03 26 40 96 22. www.boulingrin.fr. Open: Mon–Sat until late (last orders Mon–Thur 11pm, Fri–Sat 11.30pm).

Café du Palais ££–£££

A true original and part of the social hub of Reims since the 1930s. The splendidly garrulous proprietor, Jean-Louis, is an art collector and every square inch of wall space is given over to an eclectic ensemble of mainly 20th-century work. The traditional brasserie food and wine are also excellent but it's the hospitality and

atmosphere that keeps drawing locals back.

14 place Myron Herrick. Tel: 03 26 47 52 54. www.cafedupalais.fr. Open: Mon–Sat lunch (Fri & Sat also dinner).

L'Assiette Champenoise ££££

Traditional gastronomy of the highest order – see accommodation listing above.

Located at the L'Assiette Champenoise hotel, see above. Closed: Tue lunch & dinner, Wed lunch.

ENTERTAINMENT

Café Leffe

A brasserie with a bar vibe in the buzzy Place Drouet d'Erlon. Serves beers and cocktails until late.

85 place Drouet d'Erlon. Tel: 03 26 40 16 32.

Flâneries Musical d'Été

Reims' renowned music festival sees performances of, principally, popular classical music in venues across the city. There are also usually some jazz shows as well as traditional music from French-speaking African countries such as Mali. Tickets available from the tourist office.

2 rue Guillaume de Machault. Tel: 08 92 70 13 51. www.flaneriesreims.com

Le Stalingrad

A friendly, traditional *bar-tabac* and brasserie that also hosts live jazz on the first Thursday of the month in the evening. See the website for further details of gigs.

2 place Stalingrad, 180 rue de Vesle. Tel: 03 26 40 30 70. http://lestalingrad.com. Open: daily 8am–10pm.

SPORT AND LEISURE

ADA Bike rental

The bikes are provided with a helmet and a lock, for a deposit of €250.

Cours de la Gare. Tel: 03 26 82 57 81.

Publicit'Air

Hot-air balloon flights around Reims and the Champagne region.

48 rue Marcel Forestier. Tel: 03 26 36 14 82. www.publicit-air.com

Épernay and surrounds

ACCOMMODATION

Château de Juvigny ££–£££

You'll receive a charming and old-fashioned

welcome at this 18th-century château that has been in the same family for 200 years and now offers B&B accommodation. The five bedrooms (one overlooking the lake in the grounds) are all classically and individually decorated, and some are slightly rough around the edges – but that all seems to add to the charm of the place.
8 avenue du Château, Juvigny, 10km (6¼ miles) northwest of Chalons-en-Champagne. Tel: 06 78 99 69 40. www. chateaudejuvigny.com

La Villa Eugène ₤₤₤–₤₤₤₤
A beautifully restored 19th-century town-house villa that once belonged to the great Mercier champagne family (photos of them now line the walls). Set in its own grounds a couple of kilometres from the centre of Épernay, the villa has 15 lavishly decorated (Louis XVI or 'colonial' in style) rooms and suites. Breakfast is served in a conservatory overlooking the gardens,

where you will also find a swimming pool.
82–84 avenue de Champagne, Épernay. Tel: 03 26 32 44 76. www.villa-eugene.com

EATING OUT
La Grillade Gourmande ₤₤–₤₤₤
Family-run restaurant in the centre of Épernay that produces a variety of delicious fish and meat dishes from its wood-fired barbeque-grill. Has a pretty little outside terrace.
16 rue de Reims, Épernay. Tel: 03 26 55 44 22. www. lagrilladegourmande.com. Open: Tue–Sat.

ENTERTAINMENT
Le Cabaret des Secrets
A nightclub just outside Épernay that puts on fun and camp champagne-inspired cabaret performances, including burlesque acts and illusionists. See website or call for details of performance nights.
Rue des Saints-Rys, Vauciennes. Tel: 03 26 51 05 61. http://vauciennes-evenements.com

SPORT AND LEISURE
Champagne Leclerc Briant
An extraordinary (and presumably unique) opportunity to abseil 30m (98ft) underground into a champagne cellar. Groups of 15 are the minimum, but it's possible to join an existing group if there aren't enough of you.
67 rue Chaude Ruelle, Épernay. Tel: 03 26 54 45 33. www.leclercbriant.com. Open: Sept–Jul Mon–Fri 9am–noon & 1.30–5pm, Sat, Sun & bank holidays by appointment only. Closed: Aug 2nd & 3rd weeks.

Croisi Champagne
Cruises on the Marne river on the *Champagne Vallée* boat. They offer a variety of different cruise options including dinner on board. Check website for details of departures.
12 rue de la Coopérative, Cumières, 7km (4¼ miles) north of Épernay. Tel: 03 26 54 49 51. www.champagne-et-croisiere.com

Troyes
ACCOMMODATION
Comtes de Champagne £–££

Very good-value rooms are to be had in this attractive 16th-century half-timbered building with a pretty courtyard that used to be Troyes' mint. Centrally located, this is one of the best deals in the city, although bear in mind that not all rooms have their own bathroom. And ask if you specifically want a room with a bath rather than a shower.

54–56 rue de la Monnaie. Tel: 03 25 73 11 70. www.comtesdechampagne.com

Moulin d'Eguebaude £–££

Simple and basic – but charming – B&B accommodation in a mill house that is also on the site of a trout farm. There's also a restaurant serving deliciously fresh fish from the farm. Hosts are friendly and the surroundings, just west of Troyes and easily accessible by car, bucolic.

36 rue Pierre Brossolette, Estissac, 22km (14 miles) west of Troyes.

Tel: 03 25 40 42 18. www.moulineguebaude.fr

EATING OUT
Aux Crieurs de Vin £–££

A *cave* (wine shop) and atmospheric bar-bistro serving simple dishes that has an extensive wine list.

4 place Jean Jaurès. Tel: 03 25 40 01 01. www.auxcrieursdevin.com. Open: Tue–Sat noon–2pm & 7.30–10pm.

Le Bistroquet £–££

Hearty bistro-brasserie fare (including the local speciality *andouillette*, for which the establishment is particularly well known) is served at this large, popular restaurant in the centre of Troyes.

Place Langevin. Tel: 03 25 73 65 65. www.bistroquet-troyes.fr. Open: Mon–Sat noon–2.15pm & 7–10pm (Fri & Sat until 10.30pm), Sun lunch. Closed: Sept–May Sun.

East of Troyes
ACCOMMODATION
Au Rendezvous des Amis ££

Warm and friendly hotel in converted farm outbuildings in the village of Chamarandes-Choignes, just south of the centre of Chaumont on the river Marne. The spruce, light and airy rooms (with bathrooms) are full of bright contemporary décor and are very good value for money. The hotel restaurant, serving traditional regional fare with seasonal ingredients, is also highly regarded and locally popular.

4 place du Tilleul, Chamarandes-Choignes, 4km (2½ miles) south of Chaumont. Tel: 03 25 32 20 20. www.au-rendezvous-des-amis.com

Grand Hôtel Terminus Reine ££–£££

Something of a social hub in Chaumont, this is a friendly and straightforward town hotel with a decent restaurant too. Nothing fancy (and somehow all the better for it), the rooms here (all with en-suites) are simple but bright and clean.

Place Charles de Gaulle, Chaumont. Tel: 03 25 03 66 66.

Hostellerie La Montagne-Restaurant Natali £££

Probably the best B&B in the area, Hostellerie La Montagne is set in a lovely old stone house in the village of Colombey-les-Deux-Églises. All eight rooms are tastefully decorated in classic but contemporary country style. As the name suggests, the place is principally known for its food (*see below*).

Rue Pisseloup, Colombey-les-Deux-Églises. Tel: 03 25 01 51 69. www. hostellerielamontagne.com

EATING OUT
Au Rendezvous des Amis ££

Excellent little local hotel restaurant just outside Chaumont.

Located at the Au Rendezvous des Amis hotel, see above.
Open: noon–1.30pm & 7.30–9.15pm. Closed: Fri & Sun dinner & Sat.

Hostellerie La Montagne-Restaurant Natali £££–££££

This Michelin-starred restaurant (which also does B&B, *see above*) is run by a father-and-son team and has been making waves in the area. Serves classic French dishes with a fresh contemporary twist in lovely surroundings in the village of Colombey-les-Deux-Églises.

Located at the Hostellerie La Montagne-Restaurant Natali hotel, see above. Open: Wed–Sun.

Les Ardennes

ACCOMMODATION
La Cour des Prés ££

B&B is on offer at this grand fortified country house, whose owner is a descendant of the original occupier. The house was built in the mid-16th century and has impressive ground-floor rooms (which are also open to the public), with huge fireplaces and original wood panelling. Note that the house is only open during the summer months (usually Apr–Sept).

Rue Louis Martin Route de Champlin, Rumigny. Tel: 03 24 35 52 66.

EATING OUT
La Table d'Arthur 'R' ££

A very popular, unpretentious and cosy local restaurant in Charleville-Mézières with a great wine cellar and delicious and good-value dishes on offer.

9 rue Bérégovoy, Charleville-Mézières. Tel: 03 24 57 05 64. Open: Mon–Sat. Closed: Mon & Wed dinner, most of Aug.

SPORT AND LEISURE
Ardennes Nautisme

Hire out cabin cruiser boats for trips on the Meuse, Sambre and Moselle rivers.

Écluse de Pont-à-Bar, Dom-le-Mesnil, 15km (9¼ miles) south of Charleville-Mézières. Tel: 03 24 54 61 78. www. ardennes-nautisme.com

Aventure Évasion

Based deep in the Ardennes, this outfit organises all manner of outdoor activities in the area from mountain biking and trekking to canoeing and rock climbing.

RN 51, Haybes, 35km (22 miles) north of Charleville-Mézières.

Tel: 03 24 40 44 45. www.
aventure-evasion.com
**Centre Équestre des
Écuries de la Neuville-
aux-Haies**
Can organise horse-
riding trips in the
Ardennes.
*Route Forestière de la
Neuville-aux-Haies, Les
Hautes-Rivières, 20km
(12½ miles) north of
Charleville-Mézières.
Tel: 03 24 53 74 26 17.*
Philippe Lecocq
Mountain-bike and
tandem hire, and
information about
cycling in the Ardennes.
*13 rue de la Meuse,
Bogny-sur-Meuse, 12km
(7½ miles) north of
Charleville-Mézières.
Tel: 03 24 32 10 97.*

LORRAINE
Metz
ACCOMMODATION
**Hôtel de la Cathédrale
££–£££**
A charming and friendly
place in two 17th-
century buildings right
in the heart of Metz with
wonderful views of the
cathedral. The good-
value rooms are
understated and elegant
and the hotel has just the

right amount of old-
fashioned appeal without
being fusty.
*25 place de Chambre.
Tel: 03 87 75 00 02. www.
hotelcathedrale-metz.fr*
**Hôtel du
Théâtre ££–£££**
Another hotel in the
centre of Metz with views
of the cathedral. The
rooms are a little more
business-like than the
Hotel de la Cathédrale,
but there is an outdoor
swimming pool and a
decent restaurant.
*1–3 rue Saint-Marcel.
Tel: 03 87 31 10 10.*

EATING OUT
Chez Mauricette £
A lunchtime hang-out in
Metz's covered market, a
visit to Mauricette's stall
will not disappoint. Try
and grab one of the high
tables with bar stools if
you can and order a
mixed plate of charcuterie
and fromage.
*Marché couvert, Place de
la Cathédrale. Tel: 03 87
36 37 69. Open: Tue–Sat
7am–6.30pm.*
Le Bistrot de G £–££
An old-fashioned,
friendly bistro with
banquettes along the

sides and pictures on the
walls. The lunchtime
deals are very good value
but it's also a lively
evening venue and has a
good wine list.
*9 rue du Faisan. Tel: 03
87 37 06 44. www.
restaurant-bistrotdeg.com.
Open: Mon–Sat
noon–2pm & 7–10pm.*

ENTERTAINMENT
L'Arsenal
Metz's principal music
venue is set in the old
arsenal building that was
restored and remodelled
about 20 years ago. Its
programme concentrates
mainly on contemporary
classical music.
*3 avenue Ney.
Tel: 03 87 74 16 16.
www.arsenal-metz.fr*
Centre Pompidou-Metz
Check the website for
details of daytime and
evening events (such as
circus acts, music and
dance) at the gallery.
*1 parvis des Droits de
l'Homme. Tel: 03 87 15 39
39. www.
centrepompidou-metz.fr*
**Opéra-Théâtre de Metz
Métropole**
The oldest working
theatre in France has a

rich and varied season of (mainly mainstream) plays, ballet and opera.
4–5 place de la Comédie. Tel: 03 87 15 60 60. www. opera.metzmetropole.fr

Vintage

Cavern-like wine bar serving a broad but well-chosen selection of wines to a discerning crowd. Live jazz on Thursday nights adds to the Parisian-like sophistication.
14 rue des Roches. Open: Mon–Sat noon– 2pm & 6–11pm.

Sport and leisure

Chambley Planet'Air

Hot-air ballooning trips and night-glow events around Lorraine.
Hangar 610, Chambley, 25km (15½ miles) southwest of Metz. Tel: 03 82 33 73 73. www.pilatre-de-rozier.com

Nancy

Accommodation

Hotel des Prélats ££–£££

Stylishly revamped 18th-century building next to Nancy's cathedral. All the rooms have four-poster beds and stained-glass decoration. The suite at the top of the building with open-plan bathroom and exposed stonework is a treat worth splashing out on.
56 place Monsignor Ruch. Tel: 03 83 30 20 20.

Maison de Myon £££

Nancy's most chic address, this is a restored 18th-century rectory with an inner courtyard and five rooms turned out with modern yet classic sophistication (some with baths, others with showers you could get lost in). The communal rooms are spacious and welcoming places to be too – in fact, the place almost feels like a hotel, but without all the impersonality that this implies.
7 rue de Mably. Tel: 03 83 46 56 56. www.maisondemyon.com

Eating out

Grand Café Foy ££

With an address to die for, this brasserie has been serving customers for over 150 years. It may be resting on its laurels somewhat (the service can be a little lackadaisical) but the setting is fabulous, especially if you book a table by the window in the upstairs room that overlooks the square, and the brasserie fare is decent enough.
1 place Stanislas. Tel: 03 83 32 15 97. www.grandcafefoy.com. Open: daily lunch & dinner.

Le V Four £££

A tiny little place in the old part of the city on a pedestrianised street, this is where hip young locals come to eat traditional dishes with a modern twist.
10 rue Saint-Michel. Tel: 03 83 32 49 48. Open: Tue–Sun noon–2pm & 7.30–9.30pm. Closed: Sun dinner & Mon.

Entertainment

Opéra National de Lorraine

Nancy's splendid and recently restored early 20th-century opera house on Place Stanislas provides a varied programme of opera and classical music concerts.
1 rue Sainte-Catherine. Tel: 03 83 85 33 11.

www.opera-national-lorraine.fr

SPORT AND LEISURE
SPORT AND LEISURE

Maison Régionale des Sports

Lorraine's regional information office for walks and hikes.

Tomblaine, just south of Nancy. Tel: 03 83 18 87 36. http:// lorraine. ffrandonnee.fr (in French).

Verdun and surrounds

ACCOMMODATION

Hôtel Les Colombes £

A cheap, good-value 1-star hotel in the centre of Verdun. The basic rooms are clean and have all been recently redecorated; all have en-suite bathrooms.

9 avenue Garibaldi. Tel: 03 29 86 05 46.

Le Domaine de Pomone £££

Lovely B&B in an 18th-century farmhouse out in the countryside east of Saint-Mihiel. The three bedrooms are decorated in country-classic style and there's also a pretty garden to relax in.

1 ruelle de Haldat du Lys, Woinville, 10km (6¼ miles) east of Saint-Mihiel. Tel: 03 29 90 01 47. www. ledomainedepomone.fr

Château de Monthairons ££–££££

A 4-star hotel in a 19th-century manor house surrounded by a gorgeous park that stretches down to a meandering branch of the Meuse river. The rooms vary, some spacious and well appointed, others smaller and more affordable. The restaurant has a fine reputation for its expensive, gastronomic cuisine.

26 route de Verdun, Les Monthairons, about 10km (6¼ miles) south of Verdun. Tel: 03 29 87 78 55. www. chateaudesmonthairons.fr

EATING OUT

Épices et Tout ££

Friendly little restaurant that's popular with locals, serving modern, and often spicy, food.

33 rue de Gros Dégres. Tel: 03 29 86 46 88. Open: Mon–Sat lunch & dinner. Closed: Wed dinner.

SPORT AND LEISURE

Meuse Canoe

Organises canoeing trips on the beautiful Meuse river.

Charny, 8km (5 miles) north of Verdun. Tel: 06 80 22 24 18. www.meusecanoe.com (in French).

Vosges

ACCOMMODATION

Chambres d'Hôtes Breton ££

Another pleasant rural B&B in a completely restored building dating from 1720. The rooms are colourful and full of interesting furniture picked up by the owner who is an antique dealer.

Bulgnéville, 12km (7½ miles) west of Vittel. Tel: 03 29 09 21 72. www.benoitbreton.fr

EATING OUT

L'Orée du Bois ££

A good-value and quality restaurant just outside Vittel in a modern hotel designed for visitors to the Vittel spa complex. Its traditional food is elegant and delicious and the cheese board is especially good.

1 lieu dit L'Orée du Bois, Vittel. Tel: 03 29 08 88 88. www.loreeduboisvittel.fr. Open: daily lunch & dinner.

SPORT AND LEISURE
Pays des Lacs de Pierre-Percée
Watersports and other outdoor activities are based around this artificial lake in the middle Vosges.
Pierre-Percée.
Tel: 03 49 41 13 04.
www.paysdeslacs.com

ALSACE
Strasbourg
ACCOMMODATION
Hôtel du Dragon ££–£££
This family-owned 17th-century hotel has an august history and a long line of VIP customers, including – apparently – Louis XIV, the future Louis XV and Stanislas, Duke of Lorraine. The clean, contemporary rooms, some of which have views of the cathedral, belie the age of the building.
12 rue du Dragon.
Tel: 03 88 35 79 80.
www.dragon.fr

Hôtel Hannong £££–££££
A stylish hotel in an early 20th-century building centrally located near Place Kléber. The original owners were art collectors and friends of Jean Hans Arp, whose work you can see at the Musée d'Art Moderne et Contemporain in Strasbourg (*see p111*). All 72 rooms are individually decorated in sleek contemporary colours, but some are much bigger than others (hence the big range in price).
15 rue du 22 Novembre.
Tel: 03 88 32 16 22.
www.hotel-hannong.com

EATING OUT
Restaurant à la Hache £–££
This is the oldest eatery in Strasbourg and set in a gorgeous 17th-century town house on the Quai Saint-Thomas. The interior is all wood-lined and chandeliered elegance, the menu, however, is nothing fancy – just traditional brasserie and rôtisserie fare.
11 rue de la Douane.
Tel: 03 88 32 34 32.

Le Clou ££
A classic and highly respected *winstub* near the cathedral serving all the usual *choucroute* dishes and some interesting alternatives, such as calf's liver served with raisins. A cut above some of the others in this area.
3 rue Chaudron. Tel: 03 88 32 11 67. www.le-clou.com. Open: Mon–Sat lunch & dinner.

Umami £££–££££
The Japanese word *umami* can be very roughly translated as 'savoury tastiness' and it's a fair promise of what is to come inside this high-class, Michelin-starred establishment in the Petite France quarter of Strasbourg. Expect genuinely innovative, international cuisine.
8 rue des Dentelles.
Tel: 03 88 32 80 53.
Open: Mon–Fri 7.30–9.30pm, Sat noon–1.15pm & 7.30–9.30pm.

ENTERTAINMENT
La Laiterie
Renowned live jazz venue with a packed

programme of concerts throughout the year.
13 rue de Hohwald. Tel: 03 88 23 72 37. www.laiterie.artefact.org

Opéra

Home of the Opéra National du Rhin, who perform a select programme of contemporary and classic operas here and in Colmar at the Théâtre Municipal.
19 place Broglie. Tel: 03 88 75 48 00. www. operanationaldurhin.eu

Palais de la Musique et des Congrès

This 1970 building in the heart of the European quarter is home to the Orchestre Philharmonique de Strasbourg, one of the oldest orchestras in Europe.
Place de Bordeaux, Wacken. Tel: 03 88 37 67 67. www.strasbourg-events.com

SPORT AND LEISURE

Fédération du Club Vosgiene

Your first point of call for any information about hiking trails in the Vosges. The shop in Strasbourg also sells IGN hiking maps.

16 rue Sainte-Hélène. Tel: 03 88 32 57 96. Open: Mon 1–5pm, Tue–Sat 9am–noon & 1–5pm.

Northern Vosges

ACCOMMODATION

Le Clos de la Garenne £–££

A charming and very good-value small hotel and restaurant just outside the centre of Saverne. The 14 rooms (even the cheapest of which have en-suite shower/bathroom) are all prettily decorated in rustic country style. The restaurant takes its nouvelle cuisine seriously.
88 rue du Haut Barr, Saverne. Tel: 03 88 71 20 41. www. closgarenne.unblog.fr

Au Moulin de la Walk ££

Smallish hotel in a mill on the Lauter river and just outside the immediate centre of Wissembourg. The rooms, decorated in woody, Alsatian style, are comfortable and quiet and all have private bathrooms. The hotel restaurant is also highly regarded locally.
2 rue de la Walk,

Wissembourg. Tel: 03 88 94 06 44. www.moulin-walk.com

EATING OUT

Le Carrousel Bleu £££

There's a mixture of classic French dishes (like *carré d'agneau*) and interesting new takes on old favourites (*carpaccio* of duck with a pepper and nectarine vinaigrette) at this restaurant set on the river in Wissembourg.
17 rue Nationale, Wissembourg. Tel: 03 88 54 33 10. Open: Mon–Thur lunch, Fri & Sat lunch & dinner.

Southern Vosges

ACCOMMODATION

Le Colombier ££–£££

A 3-star hotel in the centre of Obernai set in a traditional half-timbered Alsatian house. Inside, the dark, wooden beams contrast attractively with the bright, modern furnishings in the comfortable rooms.
6–8 rue Dietrich, Obernai. Tel: 03 88 47 63 33. www.hotel-colombier.com

La Maison des Têtes ££–£££

Small hotel right in the centre of Colmar in a gorgeous 17th-century building. Beamed rooms are decorated in traditional – if slightly unimaginative – style, and the welcoming brasserie restaurant serves tasty, reasonably priced food.
19 rue des Têtes, Colmar.
Tel: 03 89 24 43 43.
www.la-maison-des-tetes.com

Château d'Isenbourg £££–££££

A luxury hotel and restaurant just outside Rouffach, on the wine route, with lovely views over the old town, vineyards and mountains. Set in a castle that dates from the 12th century, it has some fascinating rooms to explore (not least the cellars), and lavishly decorated bedrooms.
Rue de la Gendarmerie, Rouffach, 17km (10½ miles) south of Colmar.
Tel: 03 89 78 58 50. www.
chateaudisenbourg.com

Hostellerie de la Pommeraie £££–££££

A smart little hotel in a 17th-century abbey in the centre of Sélestat with views over the town or the hotel garden. Rooms are elegant and individually decorated, and the restaurant serves good-quality Alsatian cuisine.
8 boulevard du Maréchal Foch, Sélestat.
Tel: 03 88 92 07 84.
www.pommeraie.fr

EATING OUT

Winstub Brenner £–££

A basic and authentic *winstub* serving seasonal Alsatian dishes, with good-value *prix-fixe* (fixed-price) menus and a friendly welcome.
1 rue Turenne, Colmar.
Tel: 03 89 41 42 33.
Open: daily noon–4pm
& 7–10pm.

Aux Trois Poissons ££–£££

A waterfront restaurant, this time with a fish-based menu. You'll also find frogs' legs and other French classics, all served with a modern twist.
15 quai de la Poissonnerie, Colmar. Tel: 03 89 41 25 21. Closed: Tue, Wed & Sun dinner.

À l'Ami Fritz £££

Hearty and delicious Alsatian fare in a lovely wood-panelled dining room or on the terrace in summer. Make sure that you are very hungry before you arrive!
8 rue des Châteaux, Ottrott-le-Haut, 5km (3 miles) west of Obernai.
Tel: 03 88 95 80 81.
www.amifritz.com. Open: daily lunch & dinner.

Le Bistrot des Saveurs £££–££££

A great example of regional, seasonal cooking at its best, this 'bistro' is not cheap, but the cooking is authentic and good value all the same.
35 rue de Sélestat, Obernai. Tel: 03 88 49 90 41. Open: Wed–Sun 12.15–2.30pm & 7.15–10pm. Closed: often during holiday periods, so telephone to check that it is open before turning up.

SPORT AND LEISURE

Trace Verte

Organises hiking and mountain-biking trips in the Vosges.
7 rue des Lilas, Mutzig, 15km (9¼ miles) north of Obernai.
Tel: 03 88 38 30 69.
www.traceverte.com

Index

Acknowledgements

Thomas Cook Publishing wishes to thank MARK BASSETT, to whom the copyright belongs, for the photographs in this book, except for the following images:

AGENCE DE DÉVELOPPEMENT TOURISTIQUE – HAUTE-ALSACE 132, 133
BAINS-LES-BAINS 104
ISTOCKPHOTO 21 (Vasily Mulyukin)
MUSEE DE L'ÉCOLE DE NANCY 99
NATHANAËL HERRMANN 128
SARAH THOROWGOOD 106, 118

The author would like to thank the following people for their help, hospitality and support: Carine Buch, Vincent Jacquot and Valentine Vernier (Lorraine Tourist Board), Claude Chaboud (Picardy Tourist Board), Sarah Flook (Champagne-Ardenne Tourist Board), Catherine Lehmann (Alsace Tourist Board) and Vincent White.

For CAMBRIDGE PUBLISHING MANAGEMENT LIMITED:
Project editor: Kate Taylor
Copy editor: Anne McGregor
Typesetter: Trevor Double
Proofreaders: Ceinwen Sinclair & Caroline Hunt
Indexer: Marie Lorimer

SEND YOUR THOUGHTS TO
BOOKS@THOMASCOOK.COM

We're committed to providing the very best up-to-date information in our travel guides and constantly strive to make them as useful as they can be. You can help us to improve future editions by letting us have your feedback. If you've made a wonderful discovery on your travels that we don't already feature, if you'd like to inform us about recent changes to anything that we do include, or if you simply want to let us know your thoughts about this guidebook and how we can make it even better – we'd love to hear from you.

Send us ideas, discoveries and recommendations today and then look out for your valuable input in the next edition of this title.

Emails to the above address, or letters to the traveller guides Series Editor, Thomas Cook Publishing, PO Box 227, Coningsby Road, Peterborough PE3 8SB, UK.

Please don't forget to let us know which title your feedback refers to!